Davidson
1984

CISTERCIAN STUDIES SERIES: NUMBER ELEVEN

Cistercian Sign Language

BOARD OF EDITORS

CS 1: Thomas Merton: *The Climate of Monastic Prayer*
CS 2: Amédée Hallier: *The Monastic Theology of Aelred of Rievaulx: An Experiential Theology*
CS 3: *The Cistercian Spirit: A Symposium in Honor of Thomas Merton*
CS 4: Evagrius Ponticus: *The Praktikos: Chapters on Prayer*
CS 5: Adalbert de Vogüé: *The Community and the Abbot in the Rule of St Benedict*
CS 6: *The Rule of the Master*
CS 8: Bede Lackner: *The Eleventh-Century Background of Cîteaux*
CS 10: Jean Marie Déchanet: *William of St Thierry: The Man and his Work*
CS 11: Robert Barakat: *The Cistercian Sign Language: A Study in Non-Verbal Communication*
CS 12: *Rule and Life: An Interdisciplinary Symposium*
CS 13: *Studies in Medieval Cistercian History*
CS 14: Pierre Salmon: *The Abbot in Monastic Tradition*
CS 15: Bernard McGinn: *The Golden Chain: The Theological Anthropology of Isaac of Stella*
CS 16: Jean Leclercq: *St Bernard and the Cistercian Spirit*
CS 17: Francois Vandenbroucke: *Why Monks?*
CS 18: John J. Higgins: *Merton's Theology of Prayer*
CS 19: Jean Leclercq: *Contemplative Life*
CS 21: *Contemplative Community: An Interdisciplinary Symposium*
CS 22: Ambrose Wathen: *Silence: The Meaning of Silence in the Rule of Benedict*

CISTERCIAN STUDIES SERIES

NUMBER ELEVEN

The Cistercian Sign Language

A Study in Non-verbal Communication

Robert A. Barakat

CISTERCIAN PUBLICATIONS

KALAMAZOO, MICHIGAN
1975

Cistercian Studies Series ISBN 0–87907–800–6
This volume ISBN 0–87907–811–1

Library of Congress Catalogue Card Number 70–152476

CONTENTS

DEDICATION

IN AN AGE of great spiritual conflict and social upheaval, the monastic life seems an anachronism. Yet the role of the men and women dedicated to this way of life is as real and purposeful now as it has ever been in the past. That they have not succumbed to social and economic pressure is a credit to their unwavering faith in their vision, their ideal and their striving to attain spiritual perfection in the eyes of God and man. What they have to offer is not something material but rather an example for all men to follow, an ideal of value to all men no matter what their nationality, race, or creed. To these Christian men and women I offer this volume.

Worcester, Massachusetts
March 1972

R A B

ACKNOWLEDGEMENTS

To adequately express my thanks to those individuals who offered me assistance and encouragement during my first uncertain steps in this research project is impossible. Indeed, to compile a complete list of all those who helped is equally difficult. However, I should like to offer my thanks and appreciation to Fr Thomas Keating, Abbot of St Joseph's Abbey, Spencer, Massachusetts, and to all of the brothers of that monastery for their invaluable aid and kindness. Without them this project could not have been completed. I should also like to thank Dr Saul Cohen, Graduate Dean of Clark University, for providing the necessary funds for photographing the signs, and Mr Michael Novia for taking preliminary photographs of the signs in his spare time. The photographs of the signs in this volume are the work of Mr Benjamin McNitt whose skill is outweighed only by his patience. Through long hours of work, he always had a smile to offer and a good word of encouragement. Special thanks go to my wife, Mary, for her enduring faith in me, and my parents who have always offered assistance and encouragement.

R A B

INTRODUCTION

THE COMPILATION OF THIS dictionary of the Cistercian Sign Language is an attempt to fulfill three needs: (1) to provide an illustrated list of signs for those communities that still use them; (2) to register an historical record of this sign language; and (3) to make a basic contribution to the study of gestures, particularly technical gestures.

As a means of silent communication the Cistercian Sign Language must be studied and mastered like any spoken language. Students must have a sign list from which to draw just as students of a spoken language must have a dictionary of words. Not only will this dictionary offer a convenient source of reference for those monks who are studying the signs but it will also provide illustrations of all the basic signs.

Like spoken language, this sign language is ever changing; it is as vital and flexible as the users want to make it. More and more things are being constantly introduced into the various communities from the secular world and the brothers must have signs for them. Their options would be limited if they were confined to the official list since this has been only rarely updated by the Order. Thus the brothers invent and use signs that are not in the official listings. Individual monasteries have recognized this and have consequently drawn up local lists for use within their communities. These local lists may include items that have relevance only within a particular monastery; thus they are the equivalent of "dialect" forms in speech. More will be said about this later; suffice it to say here that these additional lists could be incorporated into the official one, thereby enhancing the sign language by bringing it up to date and making it a more adequate means of expression. At the present time so many modifications are taking place within the Order that the sign language might be completely left aside in favor of verbal communication. One way to save the signs from extinction would be to increase the inventory of vocabulary entries; the local lists offer a source of new, up-to-date signs.

The second purpose, to register an historical record of the sign language, is as important as the first. In the past, the recording of the various sign lists has often been haphazard and incomplete; incomplete simply because official lists do not represent the sign language as it is used by the brothers. The brothers are constantly making up signs where the official lists have none available. Thus, the local lists and the "original" signs are actually the language as it is used at one point in time and in a particular abbey, whereas the official lists tend to include signs which are obsolete. Some monasteries actually depend more on the local lists than on the official ones. The lists of local signs and original signs published here represent the practical attempt on the part of one monastery, St Joseph's Abbey, Spencer, Massachusetts, and its members to update the signs and make the language more useful for communication.[1]

Aside from the simple recording of these signs, one must also consider the significance of the sign language as one of numerous traditions of the cloistered life. Not only is this language used to communicate when and where speech is prohibited but it is also a reflection of the past, one of its links, as it were, with the present and future. It is only one aspect of a vast continuum embracing past customs, present changes, and future consequences. The monastic life is a life built on tradition: the habit, the cloister, the very ideals on which this life is founded. All are important because they represent interrelated and inseparable aspects of monasticism. As a part of this tradition, the sign language cannot be done away with simply because it is proving to be inadequate. It can be developed with the aid and interest of those concerned. To simply disallow the sign language in favor of verbal communication would undermine another traditional value of monasticism: *silence.*

Even though verbal communication is making inroads into the silence of the monasteries, one must recognize the significance of silence which "is indispensable for any monastic life orientated to recollection and true prayer."[2] All of the early monastic Fathers placed great emphasis on it as a prerequisite to a life without sin.[3] Indeed, "Scripture tells us that lack of control in the use

[1] The author is aware that even the official signs whose configurations are described in the *Usages* are actually made with considerable variety in the different monasteries. As it was necessary for the photographer to choose a particular monastery the oldest American community was chosen. The Spencer community traces its origins to Cistercians who came to America at the time of the French Revolution. See L. Schrepfer, *Pioneer Monks in Nova Scotia* (St. Augustine's Monastery, 1947).

[2] Order of Cistercians of the Strict Observance, *Minutes of the Sessions: the Sixtieth General Chapter*, Regional Conference, U.S.A. (n.c., 1967), p. 73.

[3] *St Benedict's Rule for Monasteries*, translated by Leonard J. Doyle (Collegeville, Minnesota, 1948), Chapters IV, VI, VII, XXXVIII and XLII all deal with some aspect of silence; see *Nicene and Post-Nicene Fathers of the Christian Church*, 2nd series, translated into English by Philip Schaff and Henry Ware, vol. XI (Grand Rapids, Michigan, 1955) for *The Institutes of John Cassian*, Bk. IV, Chapter XVII, which state that idle talk is forbidden, and so on, p. 224; *St Basil; Ascetical Works*, translated by Sister M. Monica Wagner, 2:2, (New York, 1950) also contains a number of references to silence; *The Rule of Pachomius*, Latin Text of St Jerome, ed. A. Boon (Louvain, 1932), Precepts 33 and 116, pages 21 and 44 respectively; see also the following footnotes.

of speech easily leads to sin: 'And if any man thinks himself to be religious, not bridling his tongue, but deceiving his own heart. . . . If any man offend not in word, the same is a perfect man'."[4] St Pachomius, as early as the fourth century, warns against speech at table: "If something necessary is lacking at table no one is to dare to speak, but he makes a sign to the server by a sound."[5] Likewise, St Basil (c. 329–379) enjoins novices to keep silence "because, in acquiring control of the tongue, they are at the same time giving sufficient proof of continency and, also, while they are keeping silence they will be earnest and attentive in learning from those who know how to make use of speech. . . ."[6] In the Rule of St Benedict great emphasis is placed on strict silence, so much so that St Benedict considered it an instrument of good works[7] and the ninth degree of humility.[8] Speaking, according to the Rule, is for the master; "the disciple's part is to be silent and listen."[9] Later Rules, including Caesarius of Arles (c. 470–542), Aurelius (?–551) and St Isidore of Seville (c. 560–636) also reinforce this doctrine of silence,[10] as do others in later centuries.[11]

However, this is only one aspect of the silence called for within the monastery. Another important facet of silence is that involving places and times of silence.

[4] Jas 1: 26; 3: 2, as quoted in the *Usages of the Cistercian Monks of the Strict Observance* (Monte Cistello, 1964), Bk. 8 "Silence," 254, page 62.

[5] St Pachomius, *op. cit.*, Precept 33, p. 21.

[6] St Basil, *op. cit.*, "The Long Rules," Question 13 and Reply, p. 263.

[7] St Benedict, *op. cit.*, Chapter IV "What Are the Instruments of Good Works," 52, p. 16.

[8] *Ibid.*, Chapter VII: "The ninth degree of humility is that a monk restrain his tongue and keep silence, not speaking until he is questioned. For the Scripture shows that 'in much speaking there is no escape from sin' and that 'the talkative man is not stable on the earth'." p. 27.

[9] *Ibid.*, Chapter VI, "On the Spirit of Silence," p. 20. For a full treatment of silence in the Benedictine Rule see Ambrose Wathen, *Silence; The Meaning of Silence in the Rule of Benedict*, Cistercian Studies 22 (Spencer, Mass., 1973).

[10] *The Nicene and Post-Nicene Fathers*, *op. cit.*, footnote number 1, p. 224.

[11] *Regularis Concordia*, ed. Thomas Symons (London, 1953), p. xxxviii; see also Chapter 56, pages 54–55, of this same text for regulations on silence in the reading rooms, cloister, etc.; see Ph. Guignard, *Les Monuments Primitifs de la Règle Cistercienne* (Dijon, 1878), Chapter LXXI, "Qualiter se habeant fratres tempore lectionis," pp. 172–174; Chapter LXXV, "De labore," pp. 177–180; Chapter LXXXVIII "De pena loquentium ad mensam," p. 274; and *Capitula Usuum Conversorum*, Chapter VI, "Ubi teneant silentium," pp. 281–282; *The Monastic Constitutions of Lanfranc*, ed. David Knowles (New York, 1951), "Of the Regular Silence," pp. 98–99; *Regula Pauli et Stephani*, ed. Dom J. Evangelista M. Vilanova (Abadia de Montserrat, 1959), Chapter V, p. 173.

As with the regulations against unnecessary speech, many of the Rules recommend that certain places within the cloister be set aside for silence and that there be certain times during which the religious must not presume to speak unless absolutely necessary. The places mentioned most frequently are the chapel, the cloister, the dormitory, the oratory, the refectory, the stairs and scriptorium.[12] Unbroken silence was to be kept during the time from Vespers or Compline until the next day's chapter meeting.[13] Other times include certain work periods and reading hours.[14]

Perhaps the most eloquent passage in support of silence comes from the Congregation of Cluny (910). It reveals the deep significance that silence plays in the monastic life. It is quoted here from Wolter: "The usefulness of silence is supremely necessary in every religious institute; in fact, unless it is properly observed, we cannot speak of the religious life at all, for there can be none. Silence's commendation is so great in Holy Scripture, that among the countless encomiums given to it, the great Prophet Isaiah has this to say of it: *The work of justice shall be peace, and the service of justice quietness, and security forever.*"[15]

Only in recent times has this traditional doctrine of silence been challenged and, then, only indirectly by the greater demand for verbal communication. Although speech is allowed for necessary and relevant communication, it can infringe upon the silence of the monastery if it is abused. The continued use of the sign language is necessary; the signs help maintain the atmosphere of silence so essential in a monastery. The Order recognizes the problem of too much oral communication and it has, therefore, voted to keep the signs as a means of maintaining silence.[16] Moreover, it has also voted in favor of

---

[12] G. Van Rijnberk, *Le Langage par Signes chez les Moines* (Amsterdam, 1954), pp. 6–7; St Benedict, *op. cit.*, Chapter XXXVIII "On the Weekly Reader," pp. 56–57, St Pachomius, *op. cit.*, Precepts 33 and 116; Guignard, *op. cit.*, Chapter LXXXVIII; p. 274; and Chapter VI of *Capitula Usuum Conversorum* entitled "Ubi teneant silentium," pp. 281–282; *Antiquiores Consuetudines Cluniacenses, Collectore Udalrica Monacha Benedictina* in *Patrologiae Cursus Completus*, ed. J. P. Migne, Series Latina, vol. 149, cols. 635ff (Paris, 1882), Bk. 2, Chapter 4: *Institutes of John Cassian, op. cit.*, Chapter XVII, Book IV, p. 224; see Maurus Wolter, *The Principles of Monasticism*, translated and edited by Bernard A. Sause, OSB (St Louis, Mo. and London, 1962), for quote from Congregation of Grammont, p. 50.

[13] See footnote no. 11 above.

[14] Van Rijnberk, *op. cit.*, pp. 6–7; *Regularis Concordia, op. cit.*, p. xxxviii; *Usages, op. cit.*, Book 8, Chapter 2: 258, p. 62.

[15] Wolter, *op. cit.*, "Silence," p. 50.

[16] *Sixtieth General Chapter, op. cit.*, p. 73; 114–115.

retaining times and places for complete silence. However, this is not to say that an ambivalent attitude towards the signs and verbal communication does not persist, for it does and it will doubtless manifest itself in more challenges in the future. By seeking a medium between verbal communication and the use of the signs, the Order has struck a medium between tradition and a newer, more communicative cenobitism.

One cannot say with certainty if this newer cenobitism is a threat to the monastic ideal, but one can say that it is a threat to the sign language. Since brief verbal communication was permitted about five years ago, the use of the signs among the brothers in some monasteries has decreased greatly. The possibility that the signs will be altogether eliminated in favor of speech is becoming more real each year. Herein lies the value of this book; it will stand as an historical record of an invented language, an invented means of expression, which did not disturb the silence of the cloister while at the same time providing for necessary communication. Certainly it cannot compete with speech as a medium for communicating but it did serve a very definite purpose. Its passing would be a loss because it is a link in the chain of tradition, the living reality that binds all cultures and institutions. Without the delicate chain of historical continuity most of what man knows and possesses would be fragmented and meaningless. Man looks to order and continuity in all that he does; it is no different with cloistered religious. Indeed, it is perhaps more significant since what they have is always based on what preceded them, a saint's rule, a particular monastery, or a complete ideal by which they live.

Early monastic Fathers, such as St Pachomius, and the legislators who followed him in later centuries, were obviously aware of the limitations of the signs when they allowed for speech under certain circumstances. Silence could be broken if one were in need of asking for something that required the use of speech.[17] If one could not make oneself understood through signs then speech was necessary, but it was to be reserved and brief.[18] As early as the tenth century conversations were allowed in the cloisters but only when the community was assembled.[19] During the periods of silence required

[17] Lanfranc, *op. cit.*, p. 98; Guignard, *op. cit.*, "Consuetudines," Chapter LXXXVIII, p. 274 and *Capitula Usuum Conversorum*, Chapter VI, pp. 281–282; *Regularis Concordia*, *op. cit.*, pp. xxxviii–xxxix.

[18] Guignard, *op. cit.*, Chapter LXXXVIII, p. 274; 281–282; Caesarius Heisterbacensis, *Dialogus Miraculorum*, 2 vols (Ridgewood, New Jersey, 1966), II: 21, pp. 90–91.

[19] Dom David Knowles, *The Monastic Order in England* (Cambridge, England, 1940), p. 253.

by the Rule, the *auditorium* was available for brief conversations.[20] Caesarius mentions an anecdote about two brothers who could not communicate with the signs, so they went to the Prior to speak in his presence. This is called "speaking through a third person," that is, two monks addressing themselves to someone to whom they have permission to speak in order to communicate with each other.[21] That such concessions were made in the early days of monastic orders shows that the religious legislators recognized the need for speech when signs were inadequate. Silent communication is effective only for short messages and cannot possibly be as effective and accurate as verbal communication. When speech does take precedence over the sign language it is due to the ineffectiveness of silent communication.

The third and final purpose for compiling this book on the Cistercian sign language is that it will be a contribution to the study of gestures, particularly technical gestures of which sign languages are composed. It is only recently that experts have come to realize the importance of gestures as media for silent communication, although in previous decades material has been published on some aspects of gestures, especially personal and semiotic gestures. This particular work represents one of the few attempts to study the sign language of an Order which has been using a visual system of signs for centuries and which depended upon this system to maintain silence and yet simultaneously provide a means for short, silent communication among the members. It offers a source for students of sign languages from which they may draw data for further research on non-verbal communication.

HISTORICAL EVOLUTION OF THE SIGNS

Historically, monastic signs have received little attention from scholars. There exists, for instance, no authoritative collection of signs from the various monasteries or Orders. What is available in print today, in journals and books, is a potpourri of data and literary references of varying value.[22] That such a study has not been made seems odd since there is such emphasis on

[20] *Regularis Concordia, op. cit.*, p. xxxviii.

[21] See footnote 18 above for the anecdote reference, and *Usages* of 1926, Chapter **II**, "Of Silence," for discussion of "speaking through a third person."

[22] For examples of what is meant here, see bibliographies in: Van Rijnberk, *op. cit.*, pp. 161–163; Dom Louis Gougard, *Anciennes Coutumes Claustrales* (Abbeye Saint-Martin de Ligugé, 1930), Chapter II, "Le langage des silencieux," pp. 14–23; Dom M. Anselme Dimier, in a personal letter dated October 1, 1968, informed me that very little work had been done on the study of the signs, but noted some references for me to check; see Dimier's article entitled, "Ars Signorum Cisterciensium," *Collectanea Ordinis Cisterciensium Reformatorum*, V (1950), 165–186.

silence in the writings of the early monastic Fathers,[23] as well as in the *Old* and *New Testaments*.[24] Although signs are not directly related to the ideal of spiritual perfection, they are nonetheless an integral part of the monastic life and thus worthy of study for that very reason.

Nor is this dearth of published material confined to the signs of the religious orders. The study of gestures[25] generally has been neglected for centuries. With few exceptions the main interest has been in the gestural origins of spoken language, or in finger reckoning and mime.[26] It is only within very recent decades that experts have come to realize the importance of bodily movements as culturally determined and therefore clues to the cultures themselves. Psychologists have recognized the need to scrutinize the gesture patterns of individuals as subconscious expressions of fear, defence and so on. Linguists now see that gestures are related to speech and that the verbal act of communication involves physical movements as well.[27] Such movements are the non-verbal elements of communication and are usually sub-

[23] See footnotes 3, 11, 12, and 17 above.

[24] Some *Old Testament* references are: Psalms 65:1; Zephaniah 1:7; Habakkuk 2:20; Ecclesiastes 5:1ff; *New Testament* references are: James 1:26; 3:2; John 8:47; Luke 10:39; and Matthew 4:4.

[25] For a detailed bibliography of references to studies of gestures, see Francis Hayes, "Gestures: A Working Bibliography," *Southern Folklore Quarterly*, XXI (December, 1957), 218–317; also see Weston La Barre, "Paralinguistics, Kinesics, and Cultural Anthropology," in *Approaches to Semiotics*, eds. Thomas Sebeok, A. Hayes and Mary Bateson (The Hague, 1964), pp. 191–220.

[26] Edward B. Tylor, *Primitive Culture* (London, 1903), I, pp. 163–167 and pp. 242–263; see also Tylor's *Researches into the Early History of Mankind* (New York, 1878), Chapters II, III, and IV for discussions of gesture languages, finger reckoning and mime; Florence A. Adams, *Gesture and Pantomimic Action* (Albany, New York, 1891); Sir Richard Paget, *Human Speech* (New York and London, 1930); Paget's *Babel, or the Past, Present, and Future of Human Speech* (London, 1930), Chapter I and his article, "Origin of Language, Gesture Theory," *Science*, 99 (January 7, 1944), 14–15; MacDonald Critchley, *The Language of Gesture* (London, 1939); L. J. Richardson, "Finger Reckoning among the Ancients," *American Mathematical Monthly*, XXIII (1916), 7–13; Eva M. Sanford, "De Loquela Digitorum," *The Classical Journal*, XXIII (1928), 588–593; Alexander Johannesson, *Origin of Language* (Reykjavik, 1949) and his *Gestural Origin of Language* (Reykjavik and Oxford, 1952).

[27] Ray L. Birdwhistell, *Introduction to Kinesics* (Louisville, 1952); see also his "Background to Kinesics," *etc*, XIII (1955), 10–18 and his "Some Relations between American Kinesics and Spoken American English," in *Communication and Culture*, ed. Alfred Smith (New York, 1966), 182–189; Weston La Barre, "The Cultural Basis of Emotions and Gestures," *Journal of Personality*, XVI (1947), 53; J. Vendryes, "Langage Oral et Langage par Gestes," *Journal de Psychologie*

consciously used by individuals and groups.[28] In-depth studies of the silent language of the deaf and dumb have been carried out and these constitute the most detailed and complete ones made to date on any single group.[29]

Tylor early maintained the similarity of all gesture language (languages of signs) throughout the world in all cultures and at all levels. This eminent scholar thought that the relationship between the language of the deaf and dumb and the natural language of gestures was quite easily established,[30] that, indeed, many of the signs were natural in the sense that they originated in the minds of the deaf and dumb to describe simple actions and objects.[31] Furthermore, according to Tylor, the deaf and dumb have a natural syntax or word order that is at variance with that of the spoken language and the deaf and dumb do not always want to use the latter when they communicate among themselves.[32] Given the right conditions, Tylor stated, the deaf-mutes would develop their own language of signs without the aid of the speech community at large.[33]

The argument used to counter this was first noted by Abbé de l'Epée in 1750 when he pointed out that although there was a *"langage des signes naturelles"* it was inadequate for abstract expressions. He consequently invented a system of methodic signs for abstract thought incorporating into it many of the natural pantomimic signs of the deaf-mutes.[34] Professor Stokoe, in his study of the sign language of the deaf-mutes, calls the "natural language of the signs" a myth. He bases his argument on the simple fact that very few areas of human activity are identical throughout the world, except those

Normal et Pathologique, XLIII (1950), 7–33; Jurgen Ruesch and W. Kees, *Non-Verbal Communications* (Los Angeles and Berkeley, 1956); G. W. Allport and V. Phillip, *Studies in Expressive Movement* (New York, 1933).

[28] Birdwhistell, "Some Relations," 182–189; Ruesch and Kees, in *Non-Verbal Communication*, discuss other aspects of silent communication.

[29] William C. Stokoe, Jr., "Sign Language Structure: An Outline of the Visual Communication Systems of the American Deaf," *Studies in Linguistics*, Occasional Papers No. 8 (Buffalo, 1960), pages 7–21 contain a particularly good history of the sign language of the deaf-mutes. Professor Stokoe's bibliography is also an excellent source for further, detailed readings on the language.

[30] Tylor, *Researches*, pp. 14–81; Stokoe also discusses this but more negatively than Tylor, pp. 8–11.

[31] Tylor, *Researches*, pp. 18–24.

[32] *Ibid.*, pp. 25–33.

[33] *Ibid.*, pp. 17–18.

[34] L'Abbé de l'Épée, Charles Michel, *L'instruction des sourds et muets, par la voie des signes méthodiques* (Paris, 1776); see Stokoe, "Sign Language Structure," pp. 10–11.

involving such basic activities as eating, sleeping, and so on; or "in the cases where pointing is as clear as language: *you, me; up, down;* etc. But most of the signs taken as natural, necessary, and unmistakable in the past are, of course, those parts of the total communicative activity of a culture which relates to a specific set of circumstances in that culture."[35] Professor Stokoe further notes that numerous signs have no meaning in other cultures because individual cultures have their own set of signs to which specific meanings are attached. Once removed from a culture signs determined by it might have the same configurations but not the same meanings, a rather important point since much misunderstanding might result.[36] Many sign languages have some signs in common but this in no way means that they can be easily understood among the users of them. Perhaps an example is appropriate here.

Recently this writer attended a dinner given by some friends. During the evening a young man came up to me and began to sign to me very quickly without uttering a word. Of course, I was a bit taken aback by the whole incident. When he stopped I politely enquired what this was all about. He then proceeded to propose that since he knew the sign language of the deaf-mutes, and I was studying the Cistercian sign language, why not carry on a brief silent conversation. I pointed out to him that the two languages had little in common except a few signs of a pantomimic nature and that we could not possibly carry on a conversation. It would be like speaking two different languages that have only a few borrowed terms in common. We would not be communicating at all!

This incident illustrates the fact that a natural system of signs does not exist for all cultures. It is intriguing and romantic to think that one does but not very practical. The same holds true for the gestures of the dance.[37] What meanings particular dance gestures have flow from the common consent of the members of that culture. A Westerner is not expected to fully comprehend the gesture dance of, say, India. He must first learn the meanings

[35] Stokoe, "Sign Language Structure," p. 11.

[36] *Ibid.*, pp. 10–11; see Robert A. Barakat, "Gesture Systems" Paper presented to the monthly meeting of the International Linguistics Association, New York, New York, February 8, 1969; published in *Keystone Folklore Quarterly*, XIV (1969), 110–111; Weston La Barre, "Cultural Basis," pp. 53–54; Edward T. Hall, *The Silent Language* (New York, 1959).

[37] A. Coomaraswamy and Gopalakrishnayya, *Nandikesvara; The Mirrour of Gesture*, 2nd edition (1936); G. Venkatachalam, *Dance of India* (Bombay, n.d.); A. Baram Ganguly, *Sixty-Four Arts in Ancient India* (New Delhi, 1962); A. I. Basham, *The Wonder that was India* (New York, 1959).

as determined by Indian culture. St Augustine recognized this in his day at the mime plays so popular then. He wrote: "All men, indeed, desire a certain likeness in sign-making, that the signs be as like as may be to that which is signified. But seeing that things may be like one another in many ways, such signs are not constant among men, unless by common consent."[38] Thus, the question of the "universality" of meanings of signs is answered. As will be shown later this question occurs within the Cistercian Sign Language in connection with "dialect" forms.

Before proceeding to a brief history of the sign languages in monastic orders, it is appropriate to digress here to make a few comments on the various types of gesture systems. Such systems include at least four major groups: (1) *Autistic gestures*, or those personal gestures which are quite without meaning when divorced from speech. They are directly linked to speech, to intonation and pitch patterns and serve to mark certain features of speech such as the parts of speech.[39] (2) *Culture-induced gestures*, or those specific bodily movements that are determined by and that are peculiar to the given culture of which they are a product. Such movements are learned unconsciously and used in the same manner. They are not definitely linked to speech in any real way but they can serve, like autistic gestures, to emphasize speech in some instances. Included in this group are various postures, walking (gait), nodding gestures and others which make a person, when in another culture, stand out as a person with "odd" mannerisms. One researcher has noted that culture-induced gestures can be broken down into "dialects" and "idiolects" within a specified culture.[40] (3) *Semiotic gestures* (sometimes referred to as folk gestures) constitute a rather large group of gestures that are indeed substitutes for speech. They are simple signals or symbols which have meaning only within a given cultural context and once removed from that context their meanings are altered or completely changed, although the basic configurations remain the same.[41] Included in this group are such well known gestures as the *mano fica*, or sign of the fig, *mano cornuto*, or sign of the horns,

---

[38] As quoted from Tylor, *Researches*, p. 43.

[39] Barakat, "Gesture Systems," 105–116; this four-fold classification of gestures is general at best since there are numerous sub-classes for each main group. Moreover, there is some overlapping among groups, so that each main group is not exclusive or inclusive.

[40] G. T. Hewes, "World Distribution of Certain Postural Habits," *American Anthropologist*, 57 (April, 1955), 231–244; La Barre, "Paralinguistics," pp. 195–196.

[41] Barakat, "Gesture Systems," 110–111; La Barre, "The Cultural Basis," pp. 53–57.

and the *Shanghai gesture,* or thumbing one's nose, the *social finger,* and so on.[42] Although each of these examples has wide distribution throughout the world, the meanings of each vary considerably from one culture to another. (4) *Technical gestures* as a group are limited since they are formulated by a particular group of professional people, monks, deaf-mutes, and others, to communicate silently when and where speech is awkward or impossible. Sign languages are made up of technical gestures and include those of some North American Indian tribes, truck drivers, merchants, referees, umpires and some monastic orders such as the Cistercians and Benedictines.[43] Brief, effective communication is possible with such signs by stringing them together in utterances using the spoken language as a model for syntax. Some of these groups utilize their signs in only limited communication among themselves for numbers (merchants), penalties (referees and umpires), or signals to indicate safe passing on the road (truck drivers). Most of these groups have a relatively small number of signs to express themselves. Among those who have large inventories of signs, communication can be extended and more detailed but not too abstract. Thus, if the messages are simple and brief, effective communication can be possible. Once the messages become long and complicated it becomes less likely that they will be understood.

All of the above-mentioned gesture systems are involved in some way with the act of communication, whether that be an attempt to convey an emotion, a feeling, or a more specific message. As noted earlier, autistic gestures are used subconsciously by a speaker to emphasize speech, mark grammatical elements or to convey in an unconscious manner something that they feel but do not want to convey verbally.[44] Culture-induced gestures, on the other hand, are used in more overt acts of communication and expression, such as sitting in a specific position, walking, bowing, nodding the head to indicate a negative or positive answer, all determined by the culture in which the individual user grew up. Moreover, these too may be subconscious

[42] For an excellent study of a single gesture, see Archer Taylor, *The Shanghai Gesture,* Folklore Fellows Communications No. 166 (Helsinki, 1956).

[43] Among the few articles done on these groups, see C. G. Loomis, "Sign Language of Truck Drivers," *Western Folklore,* V (1956), 205–206; D. C. Phillot, "A Note on the Merchantile Sign Language of India," *Journal and Proceedings, Royal Asiatic Society of Bengal,* N.S., III (1906), 333–334 and his, "A Note on the Sign, Code, and Secret Languages, etc., amongst the Persians," *Journal and Proceedings, Royal Society of Bengal,* N.S., III (1907), 619–622.

[44] Birdwhistell, "American Kinesics"; see Phillot's articles referred to in footnote 43 above.

acts, but with more meaning than austistic gestures within the culture; once removed from the culture there is little or no meaning conveyed in these acts. More often than not these are not related to speech.

The two groups, semiotic and technical gestures, are quite definitely linked to speech, in fact, they are substitutes for speech. Their meanings have been previously agreed upon by the group or groups that use them. Thus, they are quite arbitrary. It is also curious to note that sign languages have been invented for specific reasons, all of which seem valid and necessary within the context from which they arose. The plotters involved in the massacre known as the "Sicilian Vespers" (1282) are believed to have used a system of signs to signal when their enemies were present. Among some of the monastic orders, as already noted, there are numerous examples of sign languages invented because silence is prescribed in certain parts of the monastery and during given periods of time of the day and night, especially after Vespers or Compline until the following day's chapter meeting. This period is known as the "Great Silence" and absolute silence is the rule, except when permission is given to speak to guests and other visitors.[45] This silence is also required by rule in the refectory and other places. It is in these areas that signs are used.[46]

Other examples of sign languages are to be found among auctioneers, truck drivers, and merchants. The use of silent language among these groups is essential if, for instance, the bidding is to move quickly, or if one truck is to pass another safely. In the case of merchants, verbal communication could prove to be incriminating, or result in a lost sale. The signs they use usually have meaning only for individual groups and not for others.

Two other sign languages are of interest here. Both are "languages" in a systematic sense and are still current, although one is nearly extinct. These are the languages of the deaf-mutes and the North American Indian tribes of the Plains. The latter served as a "universal sign language" for those tribes which were from different speech communities.[47] There is some disagree-

---

[45] St Benedict's *Rule*, Chapter 42, "That No One Should Speak After Compline," pp. 60–61; see Lowrie J. Daly, sj, *Benedictine Monasticism* (New York, 1965), 206; Dom Cuthbert Butler, *Le Monachism Bénédictin* (Paris, 1924), pp. 300–303; Guignard, *Monuments*, Chapter LXXXVIII and Chapter VI (*Capitula Usuum Conversorum*), pp. 274, 281–282 and Guignard, Chapters LXXI "Qualiter se habeant fratres tempore lectionis," pp. 172–174, LXXV "De labore," pp. 177–180; Lanfranc, *Constitutions*, "Of the Regular Silence," pp. 98–99.

[46] See footnotes 3, 11, 12 above for references; also see Gougard, "Silencieux," 97.

[47] Among the better studies of the North American Indian Sign Language are the following: William P. Clark, *The Indian Sign Language* (Philadelphia, 1884); Lewis F. Hadley, *Indian Sign Talk* (Chicago, 1893); A. L. Kroeber, "Sign Language

ment about its origins but there can be little doubt that its vocabulary was enriched by extensive contact and borrowings from the language of the deaf-mutes, as Stokoe has noted.[48] Moreover, as a means of communication, it served its purpose well. Unfortunately, with the decline of traditions within the North American Indian tribes in recent years, the sign language has fallen into disuse. Studies of it are being made using rigorous linguistic methods.[49]

The second sign language, that of the deaf-mutes, has had a long history. The Abbé de l'Epée, in 1750, began his work with deaf-mutes which resulted in a method for teaching them a sign language. Incorporated into l'Épée's sign language were both the so-called "natural signs" and "methodic signs" for teaching French grammar. The latter represents "a bridge between natural signing and French."[50] Indeed, in his approach was the invention of signs for grammatical elements, function words and other signs for teaching French. His work was later carried on by Abbé Sicard, one of his students. Thomas Hopkins Gallaudet introduced this system into the United States in 1817 at Hartford, Connecticut.

Professor Stokoe designates three types of signs which correspond to the phonological, morphological, and semological levels of speech. They are: " 'natural' signs . . ., 'conventional' signs which are coinages with or without direct borrowing from another language; and 'methodical' signs, which in origin at least were sign-like labels for grammatical features of another language and were used only in teaching that language."[51] Of the three groups the latter two have contributed a few signs to the sign language of deaf-mutes but generally the first group increased its inventory through invention. Like

Inquiry," *International Journal of American Linguistics* XXIV (1958), 1–19; Garrick Mallery, *Introduction to the Study of Sign Languages among North American Indians as Illustrating the Gesture Speech of Mankind*, Bureau of American Ethnology, Introductions No. 3 (Washington, D.C., 1880) and Mallery's *A Collection of Gesture-Signs and Signals of the North American Indians with Some Comparisons*, Bureau of American Ethnology, Misc. Publications No. 1 (Washington, D.C., 1880), and his *Sign Language Among North American Indians*, Bureau of American Ethnology, 1st Annual Report (Washington, D.C., 1881); William Tompkins, *Universal Indian Sign Language*, 12th edition (San Diego, California, 1956); C. F. Voeglin, "Sign Language Analysis: On One Level or Two?" *International Journal of American Linguistics*, XXIV (1958), 71–77.

[48] Stokoe, "Sign Language Structure," pp. 14–16.

[49] Magnus Ljung, "Principles of a Stratificational Analysis of the Plains Indian Sign Language," *International Journal of American Linguistics* XXXI (1965), 119–127.

[50] Stokoe, "Sign Language Structure," pp. 11–12.

[51] *Ibid.*, pp. 13–14.

the Cistercian sign language, the syntax of the deaf-mute visual language was probably influenced by the syntax of French and later by English, although this has yet to be investigated fully.[52]

Just when a system of signs was first introduced into the monastic orders is vague and uncertain. Sign languages of many types were in use long before the birth of Christianity, in ancient Egypt, among the Greeks, and later among the Romans, who invented a system of finger counting and a language of pantomime.[53] The Venerable Bede included in his work, *De Temporum Ratione*, a method of finger reckoning probably borrowed from secular sources.[54] It is very likely that secular signs of various types had some influence on the monastic signs just as they did on the language of the deaf-mutes. Most of these signs came from the folklore traditions of some cultures. In part these borrowings from "natural" signs and from folklore tradition account for the appearance of many similar signs among the various sign languages.

There is every indication that most of the early orders specified the use of signs when and where verbal communication was not desirable. St Pachomius, for example, specified that while the millers were at work there was to be no speaking: "We must now speak about the millers. There is to be no talk, one to another, when the grain is being sprinkled with water, nor while they are kneading the dough. Likewise in the morning, they are silent except for chanting psalms or repeating some scriptural passages while carrying the loaves on the bakers' peels to the furnaces or bread ovens. Nor do they speak should they have need of some requisite; instead, they make a sign to those who can bring them what is needed."[55] St Pachomius further stated in his Rule that no one may speak while at table but must use audible signs in order to get what is needed from the server.[56] St Basil also enjoined his brethren to be silent during prescribed hours and in some places within the monastery set aside for silence. If speech was necessary, it had to be in the presence of

[52] *Ibid.*, p. 14.

[53] Eva M. Sanford, "De Loquela Digitorum," *The Classical Journal*, XXIII (1928), 589; see G. Van Rijnberk, *"Le Langage,"* pp. 7–8; Vendryes, p. 8 and Tylor, *Researches*, pp. 34–54. Anselm Dimier, "Ars Signorum Cisterciensium," *Collectanea Ordinis Cisterciensium Reformatorum*, V (1938), 165; Bruno Griesser, "Ungedruckte Texte zur Zeichensprache in den Klostern," *Analecta Sacri Ordinis Cisterciensis*, III (1947), 111–112.

[54] Sanford, "Loquela," 589; for other systems see Richardson, "Finger Reckoning," 7–13 and Tylor, *Primitive Culture*, I, pp. 246–272.

[55] St Pachomius, Precept No. 116, p. 44.

[56] *Ibid.*, Precept No. 33, p. 21.

a third person.[57] Later, St Benedict followed suit and recommended the use of signs in the refectory if anything was required. This occurs in Chapter 38, "On the Weekly Reader," and is the only passage in which the word *signum* is used. It apparently meant an "audible" rather than a "visual" sign.[58] Dom Gougard states the problem quite clearly: *Ni ici ni ailleurs, la règle ne fait allusion à l'emploi d'un système de signes manuels et visuels comme on en rencontrera plus tard dans les monastères du moyen age.*[59] However, this is not to say that a system of signs was not in use during this time. One was probably practiced, although not fixed as we see later — Cassian and Caesarius provide clues.[60]

With the foundation of Cluny (909) we begin to see the traces of a fixed system of signs emerging.[61] St Odo, who succeeded Bernon as the second Abbot of Cluny (926–942), imposed such a strict rule of silence upon his brethren that if one were to communicate it had to be through visual signs.[62] Some were then used for communication among the brothers.[63] In 1068 a monk named Bernard of Cluny drew up a list of signs totaling 296, a sizeable number which seems to indicate that many were in use before they were written down.[64] Udalricus, a monk of Cluny, also compiled a list of signs; as did William of Hirschau in 1091, basing himself on the list of Udalricus.[65] Of the three lists the latter is the longest and most detailed, giving signs for most of the ordinary things within the monastery. Included are: *les différentes sortes de pains; les légumes, les poissons, les fruits, les autres comestibles, les aromates, les liquides, les vases, les vêtements, les objets liturgiques, les choses relatives à la célébration de la messe et de l'office divin, les vêtements liturgiques, les livres usuels, les différentes sortes de personnes, d'édifices, d'instruments et d'outils et d'autres choses encore.*[66]

The earlier list of Udalricus is also interesting because of the many signs which are similar to those of the Cistercians. Among these is the one used in

[57] St Basil, *The Long Rules*, Question No. 32, pp. 295–296.

[58] St Benedict, Chapter 38, pp. 56–57.

[59] Gougard, "Silencieux," 94.

[60] *The Institutes of John Cassian*, Chapter XVII, p. 224; Caesarius Heisterbacensis, Distinction II:21, pp. 90–91.

[61] Van Rijnberk, *Le Langage*, p. 7; Gougard, "Silencieux," 93–94.

[62] Van Rijnberk, *Le Langage*, p. 9; Gougard, "Silencieux," 95–96.

[63] Gougard, "Silencieux," 95.

[64] Van Rijnberk, *Le Langage*, pp. 9–11; Gougard, "Silencieux," 95–97.

[65] Van Rijnberk, *Le Langage*, p. 10; Gougard, "Silencieux," 95; see Migne, *Patrologiae Latina*, 149, Bk. 2, Chapter 4, cols 703–705.

[66] Gougard, "Silencieux," 95–96.

the refectory for bread: *Pro singo panis, fac unum circulum cum utroque pollice, et his duobus digitis, qui sequuntur, pro eo quod et panis solet esse rotundus.*[67] Other signs similar to the Cistercians' are fish, cheese, water, vinegar and so on, but with some slight variations at times in the configurations.[68] The sign for fish imitates the movement of the fish and designates fish in general. However, the directions are quite specific if a particular kind of fish is to be signed, such as a trout: *Pro signo truitae, hoc adde ut dignum de supercilio ad supercilium trahas, propter ligaturas quae hoc in loco habentur a feminis, et quia truita semper femineo genere pronunciatur.*[69] This is the same sign used to signify woman, and is a direct reference to the type of veil worn in the middle ages in Europe by women. Chapter Three of Book Two of the Cluniac Customary in which we find Udalricus' signs, warns the brothers to learn the signs well because they can only speak rarely among themselves,[70] a further affirmation of a rule of silence that is applied not only in the refectory but elsewhere.

From the early eleventh century onward as the Cluniacs exerted more influence these sign lists were adopted by other monasteries in widely separated areas of Europe and Great Britain. For example, there are manuscripts dating from eleventh-century Anglo-Saxon England with later redactions from the thirteenth and fifteenth centuries.[71] About twenty lists are mentioned in the literature on monasteries in France, Portugal and Spain. The lists vary considerably in the total number of signs, from 55 to 472.[72] That there were sign lists drawn up for monasteries is an indication that the signs were of importance as a means of communication among the monks. They further imply that man must have a medium of expression, if not speech then a visual system. One writer puts it succinctly when he says: *Puis à ce motif psychologique, un autre s'ajoute de nature pratique; dans toute communauté d'hommes, de temps en temps il y a nécessité de se communiquer quelque chose, éventuellement pour demander du secours; c'est pourquoi en des temps et lieux où le silence est prescrit de façon absolue, les moines inventerent des signes pour se comprendre.*[73]

But the signs have their pitfalls. Giraldus Cambrensis noted an example at Canterbury in 1177 among the Benedictine monks who followed the customs

[67] Migne, *Patrologiae*, col 703.
[68] *Ibid.*, cols 703–704.
[69] *Ibid.*, cols 703–704; Gougard, "Silencieux," 98.
[70] Migne, *Patrologiae*, Bk. 2, Chapter Three, col 703.
[71] Van Rijnberk, *Le Langage*, p. 9; Gougard, "Silencieux," 96.
[72] Van Rijnberk refers to a number of sign lists of varied origins on page 11.
[73] Van Rijnberk, *Le Langage*, p. 7.

of Cluny and their strict prohibition of speech. While at table, he related, he was astonished to hear a great commotion among the brethren who, like actors and pantomimists, were gesticulating wildly and all the while whispering, yet not speaking, in compliance with the Rule.[74] St Bernard of Clairvaux, in his day, noted an abuse of the signs by the monks who readily invented "useless" signs to supplement the deficiencies in their regular list. The Saint recognized the lack of a sufficient number of signs and consequently increased the inventory to 305. The result was, of course, an enhancement of the signs for better and more effective communication.[75]

In addition to the sign language, other types of gestures are also observed as part of the ritual of monastic living, particularly in the liturgy and in prayer. Of the various liturgical postures St Augustine said: "Those external and visible bodily movements intensify the interior and invisible movements of the soul, without which they are impossible."[76] There are specified, for instance, three kinds of prostrations and other prescriptions for making gestures in church.[77] Such gestures are symbolic representations of deep religious significance inextricably bound up with the spiritual essence of Christianity and cenobitism.

WHAT THE SIGNS REVEAL

The silent language of the Cistercians is an excellent example of a system of technical gestures utilized to communicate simple messages. Such a visual system as described in this book is intended in no way to be as effective as speech, even though some of the features of spoken language are incorporated into it. The rather small inventory of signs is evidence of this. This flows from a desire on the part of the Order to restrict communication. The smaller the list the greater the restriction on communication.[78] Some of the lists available from earlier days seem to indicate that strictures on signing varied from monastery to monastery, depending upon the severity of the rule followed. It is nearly impossible to communicate when limited to only a few basic

[74] As noted in Sanford, "De Loquela," 593.

[75] Van Rijnberk, *Le Langage*, p. 11.

[76] St Augustine, as quoted in *Usages of the Cistercian Monks of the Strict Observance* (Monte Cistello, 1964), Book III, Chapter 2, "Different Liturgical Postures," p. 25; the obligation of observing these *Usages* was suppressed by the General Chapter of 1969, leaving each community free to simplify or abandon the traditional ceremonial practices and to create new ones.

[77] *Usages*, pp. 25–26.

[78] Van Rijnberk, *Le Langage*, pp. 10–11.

signs; but with a larger inventory of signs communication becomes easier and more meaningful for the brothers.[79]

Restrictions have been modified in recent times and this has resulted in an increase in the number of signs which the monks may use for silent communication. In addition, the religious invent signs quite readily to fill the gaps in the official list. Significantly, the list of "useless" signs outnumbers the authorized by about four-hundred or so. These original signs[80] serve as adjuncts to the approved list for items not included in the latter, usually newer pieces of equipment, and so on. These spontaneous signs represent an effort on the part of the monks to update the signs to make the language a more adequate means of expression, although the vast majority of these signs do not gain currency for any length of time.

As symbols, all signs, whether they be traditional or original, reflect in some way the daily lives of the brothers. The range and variety of signs is an important index to the very workings of the monastic life, its religious as well as its occupational aspects. A rather large number of signs designate the religious side quite clearly. Such things as the daily offices, prayers, objects used for rites and ceremonies, and so on, are vividly mirrored in the sign lists. Noteworthy is the fact that the religious side of the cloistered life is generally seen in the authorized list, for it is closer to the meaning of such a life, whereas the list of original signs reflects the incursions of the secular world and some of its facets.

As a self-governing and self-sustaining community, the monastery represents an interesting form of society and culture in miniature. Each of the members is required to fulfill not one office or job but many. Thus, there is an interdependence among the monks without which the monastery could not function as a religious community. This interdependence is not only religious but also economic, political and social, although not in the sense applied in the secular world. To function within the community the monks must take on responsibilities that are clearly reflected in the sign language.

[79] *Ibid.*, p. 11; Van Rijnberk has published 20 sign lists of different monasteries, ranging in number from 52 to 472; see also Mario Penna, "I *Signa Loquendi* Cisterciensis in un Codice della Biblioteca Nacional de Madrid," in *Saggi e Ricerche in Memoria di Ettore Li Gotti*, Centro di Studi Filologici e Linguistici Siciliani, Bollettino 7 (Palermo, 1962), pp. 487–521.

[80] The terms "original" and "useless" are used interchangeably by the monks as they have no sign for "original," although the former term is used in the section of the dictionary that lists the "useless" signs. They came to be called "useless" from the presupposition that the authorized list contained all the signs necessary and useful and all other signs were unnecessary or useless.

The organizational structure, complete with the various offices and officers, is seen in the sign lists. Most of the signs in this area are pure signs; that is, signs that are unique as symbols and bear no relation to speech or imitative actions. They appear to have been invented for specific use in this particular sign language. With the exception of two signs, *invitator* and *president*, all of the signs symbolizing offices and officers are unique to this sign language. Moreover, these signs are nearly all from the authorized list which indicates their age. It is unfortunately difficult, if not impossible, to trace the exact date when certain signs were invented, but there is little question that signs from the authorized list are the oldest and better reflect the traditional life of the monastery.

Among the many signs for offices and officers who make up the government of the monastery is *abbot* (touch the forehead with the tips of the two first fingers), the elected head of the community. Beneath the abbot is the *prior* (hold fist out with thumb extended upward from it) and the *sub-prior* (same sign as prior except that the little finger is also extended to indicate a diminutive). The next in the chain of organization is the *president* (extend middle finger from right fist with back of hand facing body).

Although technically not part of the governmental organization the offices of *cantor* (signs of *choir religious* and *sing*) and *deacon* (with right forefinger draw a line from left shoulder to the right hip) might also be mentioned as related to it. It is of interest to note the sign for *chapter* (join the tips of right hand in a pear-shaped configuration and touch them on the left palm which is facing down). The joining of the fingers represents an assembly of monks and the left palm a roof under which they gather as a community. The sign for *General Chapter* combines *chapter*, *abbot* and *all* to indicate the meeting of the abbots from the various monasteries within the Order.

The various occupational facets of the monastic life are revealed through the signs in two ways: (1) the authorized signs which, since they are oldest, mirror the past; and (2) the local and original signs which reflect the introduction of new objects and practices into the monastery. The lists in this dictionary reflect more specifically changes at St Joseph's Abbey because such signs are locally invented for local conditions.

Among the numerous signs from the authorized list that represent occupations, there are a number no longer in common use because less expensive secular sources provide the products these craftsmen would ordinarily make. These would include the following: *bookbinder* (*book* + *work* + *choir religious* or *lay brother*), *shoemaker* (bring closed hands together, turn them downwards and separate them sharply) and *smith* (*lay brother* or *secular* + *work* + *iron*).

Related to these signs are those that mirror some of the former pursuits of the monastic community, pursuits that were sources of income or of sustenance, which have been eliminated from the economic life of the monks because of more efficient and less expensive sources for providing them. This applies, for example, to the sign for *horse* (*animal* + pull shock or hair just above the forehead and bend head slightly). There are none presently stabled or used at the abbey because mechanized tractors are now used for cutting hay and for plowing the fields. The sign for *sickle* is rarely used nowadays because mowers have replaced it.

Just as many of the signs in the authorized list reflect the past, numerous signs from the local and original lists mirror the present. The majority of these signs are either new combinations of signs or old signs with new referents. Among the new signs are those that signify equipment introduced in recent years. Thus, *bulldozer* (*bull* + *push*), *boiler room* (*boil* + *room*), *computer* (*I* + *B* + *M*), *dump-truck* (*unload* + *machine*), *machine* (place fists together then twirl thumbs around one another several times) and *tractor* (*red* + *horse*). Other examples include *machinist* (*brother* + *work* + *machine*), *jelly department* (*sweet* + *butter* + *house*) and *refrigerator* (*cold* + *house*).

Old signs with new referents include such signs as *gasoline* (*oil* + *fire*), *plane* (*metal* + *wing*), *silk screen* (*silk* + *screen*) and *wheelbarrow* (touch the tips of both hands then move hands forward as thumbs are twirled about each other several times).

Of interest are the many signs that refer to the daily diet of the brothers. Very simple though the signs are, they are still direct reflections of the dietary practices of the monastery.

Although there are single signs for the general types of foods, like fish, bread and cereal, only those foods that are served in any variety are sub-divided into specific types. Fruits, for example, are broken down into *apple* (turn tip of right little finger into the palm of left hand), *cherry* (*red* + *grain*), *grape* (*wine* + *grain*), *peach* (lightly rub right cheek with tips of fingers of right hand), and *plum* (grasp bottom of left forefinger with right thumb and forefinger and add sign for *soft*). Since fruits are served in the refectory, and since there are no restrictions on them in the brothers' diet, there are numerous signs for the types of fruit. This is also true of vegetables. Aside from the general sign for *vegetable* (make pear shaped configuration with the left fingers pointed up, then grasp them with the right hand and add the sign for *root*), there are many signs for kinds of vegetables, once again an indication of their use in the refectory. Included are *cabbage* (clasp head with both hands and add sign for *vegetable*), *carrot* (*yellow* + *root*), *corn* (rub fists together with up and down motion several times), *beans* (*eat* + *grain*), *beetroot* (*red* or *white* + *root*), *potato* (make sign for *pear* with right forefinger) and others.

Meat and *fish* have but one general sign each; there are no sub-divisions which indicates that these are either forbidden or restrictions have been placed on their consumption in the refectory. *Meat* (pinch the flesh of the left hand just below the thumb with right thumb and forefinger), for instance, is never served in the refectory, but only to the guests of the monks in a building outside of the monastic enclosure. Thus, there is no need for types of meat such as lamb and pork; meat is not an important item in the diet. What has been said about meat may also be applied to fish, since it too was only rarely served in the refectory. In recent years, however, fish has become a regular part of the diet, but this development has not as yet resulted in any new signs for types of fish.[81]

Various types of drinks are to be noted also in all of the sign lists. The authorized list reflects the drinks previously allowed, while the local and original lists mirror the present kinds of drinks served in the refectory. In the authorized list, the signs for drinks are limited to *beef-tea* (*boil* + *meat*), *beer* (*corn* + *water*), *cider* (*apple* + *water*), *milk* (hold left forefinger with tip pointing down then grasp it with the right hand and gently pull on it as though milking a cow), *water* (join fingers in pear shaped configuration and point upward) and *wine* (place tip of right forefinger on tip of nose).

The local and original sign lists, on the other hand, include drinks that have been allowed in the refectory in recent years. These include *coffee* (*black* + *drink*), *chocolate milk* (*black* + *milk*), *soft drink* (*soft* + *drink*) and *tea* (sign for T) which has replaced *beef-tea*.

Objects of religious and liturgical significance are quite numerous in all the sign lists, particularly the authorized and local lists. Moreover, the variety of such objects is a further indication of their importance to the brothers of the community. There are, for instance, signs for the robes and cloths used during services, among which are *alb* (sign for *Mass* then pinch robe or cowl near the right knee) and *lavabo towel* (sign for *linen* then move fingers as priest does at the lavabo). Among the various objects used for the Mass are vessels such as *chalice* (*Mass* + *vessel*), *cruet* (*wine* + *water* + *blessing* + *vessel*), *thurible* (raise right hand as though incensing) and others.

---

[81] There are signs for *turkey* (*thank* + *God* + *day* + *bird*: an original sign meaning "Thanksgiving Day bird") and *hen* (*egg* + *bird*) but the latter designation refers to the hen as a source of eggs and not of flesh. Of interest as regards types of fish, Udalricus' list enumerates several types, including *salmon*, *trout*, and others, which

Of interest also are the signs used to designate the stages through which the brothers must pass before becoming full-fledged members of the monastery. The stages are few but each has a sign to symbolize it. Since these stages never change, they have signs that are included in the authorized list though all are represented in the local list as well. Among them are *postulant* (*secular* + *novice*), *novice* (put first two fingers of right hand near the right ear and add sign for *religious* or *lay brother*) and *religious* (pinch the scapular with tips of right forefinger and thumb at chest).

The signs discussed above reveal a great deal about the monastic life, the brothers' needs, diet, duties and those things which are of importance to them. However one must also note that some items not represented in the authorized or local sign lists are conspicuous by their absence. For example, one does not find "kinship terms." Blood relationships can only be signed by the use of authorized signs in new combinations with original signs or simply by original signs alone. To designate *father*, for example, one must use the qualifying sign, *secular*, to differentiate one's natural father from one's spiritual father. *Brother* must also be prefixed with either *secular* or the sign for *blood* to symbolize a blood relationship. Among the nuns *mother* and *sister* are usually prefixed with *secular* to separate them from their monastic counterparts.

NATURE OF THE SIGNS

Visual signs are, in many ways, like spoken words; that is, they are of various designations used for a variety of purposes to communicate messages through meaningful actions. Thus, the meaning of a sign must have the common consent of the community in which it is used just as words must have this prior agreement from members of the speech community that uses them. Without this consent neither signs nor words could function as elements of language, whether visual or spoken; one would have simply meaningless physical actions and sounds.

Furthermore, signs have referents in the objective world; that is, they refer to objects in the real world. This process of symbolization is much the same with words. When one enunciates a series of sounds in the form of a word then, the receiver of these sounds immediately formulates a picture of the object represented by these sounds, a chair or table, for example. The response will vary from individual to individual and the picture of the object will

seems to indicate that the monks of his monastery (Cluny) had a variety of fish to eat, for which signs were required; see *PL* 149: 703–704.

vary accordingly. Also this response will depend, to no small extent, upon the knowledge that an individual user of the words or signs has of the spoken or visual languages. One cannot expect persons to react equally to the audio stimuli of speech nor should one expect the users of manual signs to react equally to visual stimuli. In fact the reaction to the visual, as opposed to the audio stimuli, depends more on one's powers of observation.

Unlike words, however, some signs describe their object. These pantomimic signs outline the referent manually or they imitate the action with the body and its various parts. A counterpart to this in speech is the onomatopoetic nature of some words; that is, words whose sounds imitate the sounds produced in nature, *gurgling* and *bubbling*, for example. The difference between the two systems lies in the fact that the majority of pantomimic signs imitate universal actions, such as walking and swimming, whereas the depiction of sounds is valid for one spoken language only and no others. Dogs, for instance, bark differently in English than they do in Spanish or German or Arabic because of their respective sound systems.[82] This is related to the once popular theory that language arose from the imitation of sounds found in nature.[83] It has its counterpart in the gestural-origin of language which states that gesture preceded speech and that speech arose from gesture. Some scholars have noted that certain manual signs do depict universal actions and may be understood throughout the world in all societies and cultures, but they fail to note that not all actions are performed in the same manner universally, a point which shall be discussed later. Before we go on to that, however, a detailed classification of the various types of Cistercian signs is in order here.

One possible way of classifying the different types of Cistercian signs is on the basis of how they signify or symbolize their referents. There are other bases that may be used, such as physical configurations or meaning. But with physical configurations, one is confronted with a complex and cumber-

---

[82] ". . . in French, for instance, a dog does not go 'bow-wow,' but 'oua–oua,' while in Italian he goes 'bu-bu'; a turkey in France goes not 'gobble-gobble,' but 'glou-glou'; an owl does not 'hoot' but 'hulule' 's; a cat does not purr, but goes 'ron-ron'; the English mouse 'squeaks,' but the French mouse 'couic' 's." Mario Pei, *The Story of Language* (Philadelphia, 1949), p. 137.

[83] This is, of course, a reference to the "onomatopoetic" theory of the origin of language which, along with other equally imaginative theories, has been laid to rest. For brief discussions of some of these theories, see John Hughes, *The Science of Language* (New York, 1963), pp. 30–33; Mario Pei, *Invitation to Linguistics* (New York, 1965), p. 4 and *The Story of Language* (Philadelphia, 1949), pp. 14–20; Edward Sapir, *Language* (New York, 1921), pp. 4–8.

some system that is arbitrary at best since one cannot always ascertain which physical action takes precedence in a series of meaningful actions. The use of meaning is easier since one need only draw up an alphabetical list of signs according to their meanings in much the same way that a lexicographer does for a dictionary or word list. However, this method tells us little about the signs classified and nothing about how these signs signify their referents.[84] Thus, we have elected to base our classification on how signs signify or symbolize, because it seems to tell us more about the nature of these signs than the other two possibilities.

Cistercian signs, therefore, may be classified into five rather large groups: (1) *pantomimic signs*, or those signs that reproduce the actual physical movement involved or describe the object manually; (2) *pure signs*, or those signs that have no relation to speech or to imitative action but rather are unique as symbols; (3) *qualitative signs*, or those signs that assign qualities or characteristics to their referents; (4) signs that use some features of speech but are not directly dependent upon speech; and (5) *speech signs*, or those signs that have a direct relation and dependence upon speech. As with the gesture types discussed earlier, none of these groups is exclusive or inclusive because there is some overlapping from one group to another.

Some of these main groups may be further divided into sub-types with unique characteristics. Pantomimic signs, for example, may be sub-divided into (a) those signs that manually describe or outline the objects symbolized and (b) those that imitate the specific action involved in the referents. The second main group, signs that are unique as symbols but bear no relation to speech or imitative action, is more difficult to sub-classify because they are truly pure signs.

Group three, qualitative signs, may be separated into three distinct sub-groups: (a) signs that assign traits unique to the referents, usually associated qualities rather than concrete ones; (b) signs that assign concrete characteristics to the objects they represent; and (c) signs that combine both (a) and (b) to symbolize their referents. With this latter group there is some overlapping

---

[84] This writer has devised a scheme for classifying and analyzing gestures based on the parts of the body and the action involved in the gesture. It is designed in such a manner that one may analyze a particular gesture to determine all of the bodily parts and actions without regard to meaning. Moreover, the scheme may be expanded infinitely as more data became available on gestures. As a system that might be used in a field situation, however, it is quite cumbersome and may only be used as a tool for research on motion pictures of gestures or video-taped gestures. It is nearly completed but has yet to be tested as an analytical tool.

into the pantomimic signs because these signs often involve a description and then an action.

Groups four and five are interrelated in that group four uses some of the features of speech to form signs but does not depend exclusively upon speech, whereas group five is dependent upon speech, particularly its sounds. In fact, both groups clearly indicate that the monks are utilizing speech and silent communication simultaneously in much the same manner that the deaf-mutes do with the "methodic signs" discussed earlier. Moreover, most of the signs classified in these two groups are to be found in the list of original signs. To break these main groups into sub-groups is difficult because of their rather ephemeral nature; they have never been recorded nor are they used for any length of time. They exist only for a specific purpose and for a particular context. However, sufficient data have been compiled to carry out a sub-classification in regards to group four. It may be divided into: (a) signs with phonetic approximations in speech; and (b) signs that combine an accepted individual sign with an ending that is a phonetic equivalent. Group five, on the other hand, may not be so divided. It contains only signs with exact phonetic equivalents.

Group One: Pantomimic Signs. Signs classified in this first main group reproduce the actual physical bodily movements to which the signs refer. We have noted earlier that such signs represent the basic elements of most sign languages, including those of the deaf-mute community, the North American Indians and the Cistercian Order. Moreover, as Tylor and others have noted, these primitive signs represent the very rudimentary attempts on the part of the sign language users to formulate a simple medium for communicating silently.[85] Indeed, these scholars might be correct in their assumptions that these attempts further reveal the link between the origins of speech and gestic action. That gesture preceded speech is a possibility but as yet an unproven one.[86]

Furthermore, these pantomimic signs have been designated by some as "universal" signs that may be understood by anyone no matter from what culture he originates. Examples usually exhibited are *walking* (first and second fingers extended down from closed hand, then these fingers are moved one in front of the other as the hand is moved forward), *eating* (tips of first and second fingers placed on thumb of same hand then the configuration is moved

[85] Tylor, *Researches*, pp. 14–81; Grace Andrus de Laguna, *Speech; Its Function and Development* (Bloomington, Indiana, 1963), p. 6; 13–14; 112–116.
[86] A number of scholars have suggested a gestural origin of speech, among whom Alexander Johanneson is outstanding; see footnote 26 above for references.

back and forth toward the open mouth), *sleeping* (palm of hand or hands are placed on one side of the head and then the head is tilted to one side as though resting on a pillow) and others of a similar nature. There indeed may be a few universal signs among many cultures but this in no way accounts for the rather large number of signs that depict other so-called universal actions. Pointing to indicate something at a distance varies from culture to culture; in the West the forefinger is generally used while in some parts of the world the lips are used. Gestures for waving goodbye vary as well; in Greece and the Middle East, including most of the Arab countries, one waves goodbye with the palm facing oneself and the fingers are moved back and forth as though beckoning, while in England and the United States the palm faces forward and the fingers are moved forward slightly either together or rapidly one after another. Nodding to affirm or negate also is a so-called universal sign but it too varies considerably from culture to culture; a problem that vexes many a traveller in such places as India where the nod of affirmation is similar to the Western nod for negation.

Mime, in particular, offers a good illustration of the false assumption that there are great numbers of universal signs or actions. If mime were universally understood, then there would be no need for manuals to explain gestures used in mime. Westerners would not be bewildered by the subtle meanings of gestures in the Indian dance if actions were universally understood, but they are in fact bewildered.[87] What this school of thought fails to account for is that even basic bodily movements are culturally determined; that is, the movements themselves and their meanings, if any, are determined by the cultures that produce them.[88] Once removed from these cultures the meanings of the gestures are lost or, as the case may be, misinterpreted by alien observers.

Perhaps a brief linguistic analogy between the sounds of speech and the physical configurations of manual signs will clear up this question of universality.

The sounds of language are like the physical configurations of manual signs. A single sound, may have meaning or, when combined in various structures with other sounds, it may help determine the unique meaning of that par-

---

[87] Some excellent Indian dance manuals and studies are: Vidya Sarabhai Nawab, *419 Illustrations of Indian Music and Dance in Western Indian Style* (Ahmedabad, 1964); Enakshi Bhavani, *The Dance of India* (Bombay, 1965); Faubion Bowers, *The Dance in India* (New York, 1953); see also footnote 37 above for additional references to Indian dance.

[88] La Barre, "Cultural Basis," 53–56; Hewes, "World Distribution," 241–242; Barakat, "Gesture Systems," 110–115.

ticular group of sounds. It is the same with manual signs and the physical configurations which comprise them. A configuration may stand alone and have meaning, or it may be combined with other configurations to contribute to the unique meaning of that group of gestures. Remove one physical configuration and the meaning may change or be lost altogether. For a given language, therefore, whether spoken or silent, certain sounds and physical movements must be commonly accepted so that meanings may be determined. The fact that languages share some common sounds and physical configurations is interesting but of relatively little importance; what is significant is the meanings attached to these basic elements and how they are compounded. Though some spoken languages have similar sounds they do but rarely attach the same or even similar meanings to them. Likewise with sign languages and their physical gestures. The cultural contexts determine the meanings.[89]

Pantomimic signs constitute a large segment of the total number of signs in the authorized list presented in this book. These imitative signs may be the most "primitive" signs because they represent a level of silent communication that is the simplest. Such signs require a single action akin to the actual movement in the objective world of a given culture or a manual description of an object of simple design or construction. They are the oldest ones in the Cistercian sign language and have been in the sign inventory since the inception of the language itself. They were the obvious beginnings of silent communication because they are the most natural and least complicated in physical movement and meaning.

Such signs, of course, are not confined to the sign language of the Cistercian monks but are used in the secular world as well. When a man has been fishing and later wants to tell his friends about the size of the fish he caught, he will most likely hold out his hands in front of himself to indicate its length. He might also want to describe its girth by holding the tips of his forefingers and thumbs in close proximity to form a circle. Furthermore, he might want to show his audience just how he caught the fish; that is, the struggle he went through to "hook it," "reel it in" and "net it." To illustrate each of the steps, he might attempt to reproduce the actual movements he had to go through to get it into his creel. No words need pass between or among the men: the substance of the message could be made clear through imitative action.

Monks do the same thing when they manually outline a table, or pantomimically represent the act of running or eating. They are, in essence,

[89] Birdwhistell, *Introduction to Kinesics*, pp. 5–13; also see his "Background to Kinesics," 10–18 and "Some Relations between American Kinesics and Spoken American English," 182–189.

depicting or describing the action or object with their body movements or hands. A table, for example, is described manually with two hands, palms down, moved in opposite directions as though indicating a table top. To describe a bed, they simply add the pantomimic sign for *sleep*; thus, we have two pantomimic signs compounded to form a sign for *bed* (*sleep + table*).

These signs may be considered basic elements of the Cistercian sign language in that they are the most easily understood of all the sign types. To those brothers whose grasp of this visual system of communication is tenuous, these signs are understood with little trouble because they are quite concrete. When a message becomes more complex and more abstract, some of the brothers have greater difficulty comprehending it; their grasp of the signs may not be adequate. On the simpler, pantomimic level of communication, this difficulty is overcome by the simplistic nature of these signs.

As noted earlier, pantomimic signs may be sub-divided into two sub-groups: (a) those signs that manually describe an object; and (b) those that imitate a specific action. Members of this first sub-group include signs like *book* (hold palms of hands together then open them with heels of hands held together as though opening and closing a book), *basket* (describe a horizontal circle in front of body with right forefinger then lift hands as though grasping the handles of a basket), *cross* (hold left forefinger vertically then place right forefinger across it to form a cross), *hook* (curve right forefinger like a hook and hold hand up above right shoulder), *house* (form a roof with tips of fingers of both hands) and others too numerous to list here.

The second sub-group of pantomimic signs involves an imitation of a specific action. These imitative signs reproduce with the hands and body actions that relate to the monastic life and the myriad number of chores that the monks must perform at one time or another. Included are signs like *dig*, *mow*, *pray*, *work* and so on. Also included are signs for some of the tools used to carry out these actions such as *sickle* and *shovel*.

Like other types of signs in the Cistercian sign language, some of the signs of sub-group two may be used interchangeably as either nouns or verbs, depending upon the context in which the signs are used. For example, the sign for *milk* may be used to refer to milk or to the act of milking. In either situation, the imitation of the act of milking is significant. *Butter*, although officially a noun in the authorized sign list, is used as a verb on occasion.

Other signs of this sub-group have more than one referent; that is, these signs may be used in alternate contexts for related things. *Discipline* may also symbolize *penance* and *sickle* symbolize *cut*. Each of these examples is pantomimic and basic to the sign language.

Group Two: Pure Signs. The second main group of signs, designated as pure signs because they are true substitutes for spoken language, is composed of signs that bear no relation to speech or pantomimic action. As unique products of the monastic community, these signs derive their significance from the culture of that community; that is, they symbolize items, objects, offices, practices, and so on, that are peculiar to this particular group. If applied to similar things beyond the confines of the monastery, they either lose their unique meanings in some manner or they take on different referents.

These signs, as true substitutes for speech, are an attempt to develop a sign language on a more abstract and efficient level. Since there is no dependence on speech sounds as regards form or meanings, the referents may be thought of as unique symbols. Most of the pure signs were apparently invented to signify things for which no natural signs existed. The sign for *abbot*, for instance, is made by placing the tips of the right forefinger and middle finger on the forehead so the tips of the fingers are pointing up. This configuration refers to the abbot only and cannot be confused with other signs of the language either in the actual physical arrangement of the fingers and hand or in meaning. Moreover, the act of placing the fingers on the forehead does not represent any article of headgear that abbots wear, so the sign in no way ascribes a characteristic or quality to the referent. This is also true of the signs for *animal* (curve right forefinger and place the middle joint on the tip of the nose then move the finger over the nose-tip several times), *day* (place tip of right forefinger on right cheek), *prior* (hold right thumb up from fist), *rule* (rub right palm or fingers on little finger side of left hand), and the various colors, such as *green* (with tip of right forefinger draw a line from the right ear to tip of nose), *purple* (place right forefinger and middle finger on forehead so that fingertips point to the left), *yellow* (with tips of right forefinger and middle finger draw a line from between eyebrows to tip of nose). Red appears to be the only sign that might attribute a quality to its referent by touching the lower lip with the tip of the right forefinger, the one part of the face that is red. The other signs for colors are strictly arbitrary in nature.

Two of these pure signs are curious because they represent the only ones in the group that have equivalents in the secular world. Both *invitator* and *president* are designated by signs that have been traditionally associated with secular signs, *mano fica* (thrust thumb between forefinger and middle finger of same hand) in the case of the former sign and the *social finger* (hold middle finger out from tightly held fist) in the latter. Neither of the two signs, however, have retained secular meanings, even if they were introduced into the sign language from the secular world. One must consider them pure signs because they have unique significance to the brothers.

Group Three: Qualitative Signs. Qualitative signs, so called because they assign qualities, traits or characteristics to their referents, represent a stage in the evolution of the sign language that is roughly comparable to metaphor or connotation in spoken language. This simply means that the referents are defined in terms of what qualities are associated with them. For examples one need only look at the signs for various nationalities or the signs for the Cistercians and Benedictines. Each is defined by what the monks traditionally associate with them, particular features such as diet, dress or a feature popularly associated with the homelands of various nationalities. Such signs define their referents in terms of something else that is more figurative in nature than a simple, direct denotative sign.[90]

Signs within this group may be classified in three sub-groups, as noted earlier. The first sub-group includes signs which assign traits unique to the referents, but usually abstract ones rather than concrete traits as is the case with sub-group two. Within this first sub-division, therefore, we find signs for nationalities, some countries, cities and numerous Biblical characters, places and events. Holy days are also represented in this sub-group.

Nationalities are particularly interesting because the signs symbolizing them can reveal when the signs were introduced into the sign language and what traits the monks associated with these nationalities at that time. The influence of the popular attitudes and connotations are present. The Irish, for example, are designated as *green* or *potato eater*(s). The former sign is a direct reference to Ireland as the Emerald Isle or the color popularly associated with the Irish and Ireland. The latter sign, on the other hand, refers to a traditional staple of the Irishman's diet. Englishmen are identified as *biscuit eater*(s) or they might be designated as simply *biscuit*, a food popularly associated with Englishmen.[91] The sign for *spaghetti* is used to define the Italians, while Americans have: *yank + key*. A handlebar moustache is alluded to in the sign for German since one twists thumb and forefinger of both hands on either side of the upper lip as though twisting the ends of a moustache. With the exception of the sign for *Chinese*, all of the above signs are placed in the list of original signs.

Signs for countries operate on much the same level as those for nationalities,

---

[90] We have elected to use the term metaphor here because it seems most appropriate. However, one might also use connotative as well since the signers create signs for things in terms of what they associate with them.

[91] An alternative sign for Englishman is *t + drink*, although it is only rarely used.

except that they refer to a physical or political entity in most instances. *France*, for example, is signed as *f* + *tongue* (hold tip of tongue with thumb and forefinger) + *courtyard* (hold extended forefingers in front of body with tips down then move them in a semi-circle to sides of body). The letter *f* means French, *tongue* is language and *courtyard* is the country implying both a physical and a political entity simultaneously. In the same manner, *England* is signed as *e* + *tongue* + *courtyard*, or as *drink* + *t* (*tea*) + *courtyard*, the first sign indicating that this is the country where English is spoken (as with *France*) and the second alludes to the fact that it is also a country in which tea is a popular drink. *Africa* is identified as *black* + *courtyard*, the continent whose inhabitants are black. *Russia* is signed as *red* (place tip of right forefinger on lower lip) + *courtyard*, a reference to a political slang expression meaning communist. However, in terms of the Cistercian sign language and the cenobitic life, this designation is not derogatory as it is in speech. One should also note in passing that nationalities may be identified by the use of these signs for countries simply by adding the sign for *secular* (pass the side of right thumb over lips and chin) in the terminal position. Thus, *Russian* is signed as *red* + *courtyard* + *secular* which means literally a person from this communist country. Although this particular formula for designating nationalities is usually superseded by individual signs, it is occasionally used when no single sign is available.

Cities, biblical characters, places and events, as members of this sub-group, are identified by what event took place there, who was involved or where the event took place. Since there are no signs in the authorized list for cities, the brothers have had to use their ingenuity to invent them when necessary to identify these referents. Like the various signs for biblical characters, places and events, signs for cities are found only in the list of original signs. Some cities may be signified by their initials, as *n* + *y* for New York City ro *l* + *a* for Los Angeles. To fully understand these particular signs one must have an excellent grasp of the context in which the letters are used. On the other hand, some cities are identified by a famous event or person associated in some way with them. For example, Dallas Texas, in the sign language is: *secular* + *courtyard* + *president* + *K* + *shoot*, or *secular* + *courtyard* + *shoot* + *president* + *K*. Thus, the fact that President Kennedy was assassinated in Dallas becomes that city's associated or identifying element. Washington, D.C., is signed as *president* + *courtyard*, or the city in which the President of the United States of America lives. Rome is simply *Pope* + *courtyard*. Note that in these examples *secular* is used for cities not associated with religion, whereas this is not used when defining Rome, the city most often associated with the Pope.

Signs for Biblical characters and events are composed of single or compound signs of various types. However, the end results are designations of a highly figurative nature which oftentimes border on the metaphoric. Nearly all of these signs are from the original sign list which seems to indicate brief currency and personal usage; that is, these signs are invented within and for a particular context by an individual for a specific purpose. Once removed from that context the sign loses its contextual significance and would doubtless require another series of signs differently arranged depending, of course, upon the signer and the context.

To formulate signs for Biblical characters and events requires an intimate knowledge of basic signs, ingenuity and imagination, and familiarity with the *Bible*. Of course, the person to whom these signs are made must also possess these; if not, the signs would doubtless be meaningless. Although there is no specific designation for Bathsheba in the sign lists, one may sign her name by simply associating her husband, King David, with signs for her outstanding qualities. Thus Bathsheba is signed as *beautiful + lady + marry + psalm + king*, the first two signs indicating qualities, the third an act, and, finally, the last two identify King David.

Examples of places from the *Bible* also are interesting. The river *Jordan*, for instance, is signed *water + road + close + two + God + book + courtyard*. Signs one and two designate *river*; signs three and four indicate an approximate location and, finally, signs five, six, and seven signify the Holy Land. Thus, the sign for the River Jordan literally means "the river which ran near the Holy Land where the events of the Bible took place." Nazareth offers another excellent example of a sign which identifies its referent by an event or character identified with it. Like the River Jordan, and others, *where* is implied in this sign for Nazareth. The sign is *secular + courtyard + cross + God + hide + three + zero + year*. We have then "city (secular courtyard) where Jesus (cross God) stayed (hide) for thirty years (three zero year)." *Sodom* presents a complex association of events and persons: *bad + secular + courtyard + burn + time + lady + change + two + salt*. Translated into speech the sign means "the evil city that was burning when the lady was turned to salt." The first segment of this sign serves to identify the city but it is the latter part beginning with *time* that serves further to qualify the first segment by associating a person and an event with it. Numerous other examples are to be noted in the sign lists, but those above are representative.

Holy days and seasons, like other signs within this first sub-group of qualitative signs, are designated by associations. *Holy day* itself may be signed in one of three ways: (1) *big + useless + day*; (2) *no + work + day*; and (3) *saint + day*. *Easter* is simply *God + up + day*,[92] or in a more popular sense, *egg + day*. *Lent* is signed as *big + fast + time*; and *Christmas* is *baby + God + day*. Seasons, such as *summer*, are also identified by what is associated with them in the minds of the brothers. *Summer*, for example, may be designated as *hot + time*, whereas *fall* prefixes the sign for *end* to the signs for *summer*; thus, *fall* becomes *end + hot + time*. Oftentimes qualifying signs may be added to better identify the referent to the observer.

Sub-group two, those signs that assign concrete traits or qualities to their referents, tend to be less abstract and personal, more specific. There is, therefore, a more direct relationship between the sign and its referent through a concrete identification of a quality or trait. In this respect, signs within this particular sub-group are used to identify some monastic orders, objects of religious significance, some metals and a few drinks. Of course, these are only representative examples since other signs for different things may also be included in this second sub-group.

Cloistered orders, like the Cistercians and Benedictines, are designated in much the same manner as in speech. In speech, both orders are signified by the colors of their respective habits, at least popularly. Therefore, the Cistercians are the "white monks" and the Benedictines the "black monks." When translated into the language of signs, the latter group is similarly described as the *black + monk*; the former as *white + monk*. Sometimes the designation, *monk*, is used without qualification because when the sign is used in the monastery the referent is understood.

Among the many objects of religious significance that assign concrete traits to their referents are the following: *altar*, *altar-cloth* and *host*. To sign the former object the signs for *Mass* and *table* are combined, the first sign specifying the thing done at the altar. *Altar-cloth* combines the signs for *altar* and suffixes the sign for *linen*. The signs, *Mass* and *bread*, serve to designate *host*, *bread* being the significant element here.

Some metals are signified by their characteristic colors. *Copper*, for example, is signed as *red + metal*,[93] while *silver* is *white + metal*. Likewise, some liquids may be designated by their colors, such as *coffee* (*black + drink*) and *ink* (*black + water + write*).

---

[92] This combination of signs means that "God rose from the dead on this day," or "God is risen." One must be careful not to confuse this sign with the Ascension.

[93] The dialect form of this sign does not include *hard*; thus it is listed in the local list as *red + metal*.

Frequently, liquids may be conceived of in terms of what fruit they are made from. Thus, *cider* is signed as *apple + water*,[94] and *beer* as *corn + water*.[95] *Vinegar* is identified by its sourness as well as what it is made from: *sour + wine*.

Those signs that combine sub-groups one and two comprise the final sub-division of qualitative signs. As mentioned earlier, there is some overlap into pantomimic signs because this sub-group sometimes includes signs with a description or an action as one of the elements. Thus, the sign for *pond* is signed as *fish + water*, the former sign being a pantomimic sign. *Pen* is similar in that it combines both an action and a quality; thus, *wing + write* represent a quality (*wing* is a reference to the quill pen) and an action (*write* is a reference to the act of writing). *Pencil* incorporates an action sign and a specific characteristic of pencils: *wood* is the qualitative sign while *write* is the action sign. *Procession* uses a sign that outlines an object (*cross*) followed by an action sign (*go*), both of which serve to designate a characteristic of the referent.

Group Four: Signs partially dependent on speech. Signs classified in this major group offer a great deal of interesting material for study by linguists. These signs seem to represent a stage in the development of the sign language that links the visual system with speech and some of its features. As will be shown later this link becomes clearer with signs completely dependent upon speech. What reasons there are for this increasing dependence on speech remain obscure. However, some comments are appropriate here because they should clarify some characteristics of both groups four and five.

Since the Cistercian sign language was never intended to expand communication among the brothers but rather to restrict it to some extent, the administration of the Order has rarely seen fit to increase the sign inventory for fear of intrusion upon the traditional silence and meditative atmosphere in the monasteries. Thus, there has always existed a restrictive vocabulary in this sign language. To make up for this insufficiency, the monks have come to depend more and more on speech in inventing signs to fulfill an immediate need in a particular context. These so-called "useless" signs are often directly related to speech in that they utilize certain features, specifically phonetic qualities, of speech already in the signer's mind and which hopefully will be understood by the receiver who must also have them in his mind as well.

---

[94] An alternate sign for *cider* is the speech sign composed of two phonetic elements, *side + r*. The presence of this alternate sign indicates that two signs for the same referent can and do persist in the sign language.

[95] The sign for *beer* may also refer to *ale* in some contexts.

When signers do create signs related to spoken language, they are, in a manner of speaking, translating sounds to their manual equivalents.

This is, of course, possible since the cloistered monks are operating with two communication systems: speech and silent language, the latter system dependent upon the former to some extent. Deaf-mutes do not have this advantage because they have only the visual system available to them, although there is growing use of lip-reading that may or may not be affecting their sign language. Therefore the deaf-mute sign language is not dependent upon speech in the same way that the Cistercian sign language is. What relation the deaf-mute language bears to speech is artificially and consciously applied.

Not so with the monks; they apparently create signs with links to speech by a sub-conscious series of relationships, naturally and quite ingeniously determined. Such relationships are somewhat akin to alphabets as graphic representations of the sounds of speech. Thus, when we see a particular letter we equate it with a particular sound, at least in our minds. The only difference between this type of association and that made by the monks is that with the latter the association is made between sounds and signs rather than between written letters and sounds. What they are essentially attempting to do is to "speak through signs," using their native language as a point of reference.

The fact that they are using their native language as a point of reference implies that the signs which depend upon speech either partially or completely have no meaning beyond the speech community of which the brothers are members. Thus, if signs which use some features of speech or rely completely on some speech features to convey meaning are transmitted from an American monastery to a French monastery they will lose their significance altogether. Different sound systems in English and in French are the critical factors. Just as one would not expect an English speaker to communicate with a French speaker if they did not know each other's languages, so signs dependent upon specific language sound systems may be used only with persons who know these systems.

Even then, sign languages, like spoken languages, tend to form "dialects." Signs in group four and five are in many ways dialect forms of the sign language that have been translated from spoken dialect forms. Oftentimes they exhibit all the peculiarities of speech, depending of course, on the individual group and its members and how they perceive and use speech. Within a given language community, these signs are frequently not understood by persons from other dialect areas even though all use a system of signs that is based on standard signs. These dialects become a barrier to the formation of a "universal" sign language for the Cistercian monks because the forms developed are quite divergent and may be understood only by the members of the community which created them. Moreover, since monks do live in a close-knit, homogeneous micro-culture, they invent and understand not only dialect forms but also "idiolect" forms that are highly idiosyncratic in nature. Through a long process of adjustment and assimilation into that culture, an intimacy evolves not unlike one might find among the members of a family. Indeed, like members of a family, monks do communicate non-verbally with gestures other than those in the sign language. They have come to recognize certain idiosyncratic movements and they have attached meanings to them even though no explicit agreement has been reached between or among them as to specific meanings.

It is also curious to note that nearly all signs related to speech sounds are short-lived. The conditions under which these are invented give significance to them. When introduced into a different context they lose their meanings or, at least, have them modified. Some of these signs are slang terms that are closely related to their verbal counterparts. A few such signs do become fixed and reveal the period when they were adopted or adapted, especially if their speech equivalents have died out. Limited contact with the ever changing secular world and its changing languages has created a situation in which older forms can survive and possibly flourish, albeit unofficially.

Sub-group one of this main class of signs includes signs that have approximate phonetic equivalents in English. Oftentimes these signs bear no relation to the new referent except in sound and then only superficially. Thus, a brother may sign *read* and add a suffix, *e* or *y*, to form *ready*. Other examples are: *baloney* (*bull* + *o* + *knee*); *Ceylon* (*c* + *long*); *Hawaii* (*high* + *y* + *e*); *Dakota* (*d* + *coat* + *a*) and numerous others. Note that the initial syllable, *ba-*, is signed as *bull*, a close approximation at best, whereas the latter two syllables are more exact. The *c* in *Ceylon* is nearly exact but the *long* falls far short as a representation of *-lon*. *High* in the next example is a not too successful attempt at approximating the initial segment of *Hawaii* as also the *d* for *Dakota*, but *coat* and *a* carry their phonetic burdens well.

The second sub-group of group four has been distinguished from the previous sub-group on the basis that the initial sign in the combined form may not be used to represent any new referent; it must stand for itself only. In addition, a suffix with a phonetic equivalent in speech is added to this first sign. When signers are forced to formulate *-ing* or *-en* forms, they simply add the letter *n*. Hence, *harden* is signed as *hard* + *n*. *Going* is similar in that *n* may be suffixed to the sign for *go*, as *n* may be added to *walk* (*walk* + *n*) to form *walking*. The letter *r* may be suffixed to some forms to make *-r* or *-re* endings, as in *older* (*old* + *r*); *filler* (*fill* + *r*); *singer* (*sing* + *r*) and so on.

Adjectives are made by suffixing the signs for *knee* (touch side of right knee with right hand), *e* or *y*, depending upon the initial sign's sounds. Thus, we have *shine* + *knee* (or *e*; *y*) to form *shiney*; *fun* + *knee* (or *e*; *y*) to form *funny* and *corn* + *knee* (or *e*; *y*) to make *corny*.

Group Five: Speech Signs. Signs classified in this main group have exact or nearly exact phonetic equivalents in speech sounds. Unlike the signs in sub-group two of group four, these signs frequently are used to signify different referents on the basis of what sounds are referred to in an utterance. Thus, the sign for *deer* (place thumbs on sides of head then spread fingers) is used to designate *dear* because their sounds are similar in the participants' minds. *Sew* (place tips of right thumb and forefinger together and run over first two fingers and thumb of left hand as though sewing) symbolizes *so*, as does *two* for either the preposition *to* or the adverb *too*.

Many of these signs are found in the list of original signs and they represent attempts to create signs for things in the secular world for which there are no signs in the official list. These invented signs can be highly imaginative and sometimes difficult to understand. To fully grasp their meanings requires a mental agility and imagination equal to that of the signer. When a signer expresses the following sequence, the receiver of the message must be aware of things beyond a simple series of signs; he must "see" and "hear" the utterance. Thus, *sin* (hit chest with right hand) + *sin* + *a* + *t* refers to the city of Cincinatti, Ohio, not because *sin* has any part in determining meaning but because *sin* has the appropriate phonetic value for the signer and the observer. Indeed, *Ohio* is signed as *o* + *high* (hold right hand overhead with palm down) + *o*, an equally imaginative, if not ingenious, sequence of signs. Similarly, the signs for *I* or *me* and the letter *m* are combined to form the contraction, *I'm*. The letter *v* and the sign for *key* are also exploited for their phonetic value to form signs, such as *day* + *v* to make *Dave* but really representing *David*. *Key* occurs occasionally as an ending for signs like *cookie* (*cook* + *key*) and *yanky* (*yank* + *key*).

Although this group of signs is small in number compared to the other four groups, they do represent a complete dependence on their phonetic qualities in the minds of the participants. They further illustrate a stage in the development of the Cistercian sign language that establishes a final link between the visual and sound systems. Their use implies that the brothers actually conceive of these signs in terms of both the visual and the phonetic.

Since these people have each system at their command, they are able to utilize them imaginatively and ingeniously for whatever effects they wish to create.

MORPHOLOGY OF SIGNS

One of the most interesting aspects of the Cistercian sign language is the means used to compound signs; that is, the methods for combining single signs into signs with two, three or more elements. As with syntax, signs are compounded with spoken English patterns as models, or any of the spoken languages with which the monks communicate in a particular monastery. Thus, French patterns would be used in a French monastery, and so on. This is a problem that will be discussed later under the section on syntax and it does have a bearing on the so-called "universality" of the signs.

Signs may be classified into two major classes for purposes of discussing morphology: (1) *basic*; and (2) *derived* signs, with this latter group sub-divided into two sub-groups: (a) *simple*; and (b) *compound*. Basic signs are those signs with a single element, such as *book* and *little*. Derived signs are composed of more than one element. These may be separated into simple signs, those with two or three elements, usually basic signs, such as *snow* (*white* + *rain*); and compound signs, or those signs with four or more elements, such as *decide* (*arrange* + *head* + *before* + *time*), *grow* (*arrange* + *vegetable* + *two* + *come* + *up*), and *star* (*little* + *night* + *time* + *light* + then point up to sky with right forefinger). More complex examples of this type will be discussed later in this section.

Basic signs are the least complicated of the sign types classified here. They are the simplest because they contain a single element only, involving usually no more than one, and rarely, two gestures. In rather simplistic terms basic signs are the building blocks for other, more complicated signs with a greater number of elements. In addition, their referents are objects, acts, or segments of time and simple measurements. We have noted some examples above, i.e., *book*, *little*, but there are numerous others such as *house* or *room*, *broom*, *fork*, *glass*, *key*, and *tongue* or *language*.

All of the above noted examples represent objects or things. Acts may be designated by basic signs also. Some basic signs describing acts are *dig*, *eat*, *give*, *saw*, *sweep* and others. Some of these signs representing acts may also refer to the object used to perform them, as *saw*.

Segments of time and simple measurements are indicated with some of these basic signs. To designate future, for example, a simple movement of the right hand forward from the right shoulder is made; this same gesture is also used to symbolize *before*. *After* and the simple past tense may be made by a movement of the right hand backwards over the right shoulder or backwards from hip level with the palm facing the rear. *Counting* (hold out left hand with fingers spread then touch them with the tip of the right forefinger as though counting on the fingers) and *little* (place tip of right forefinger on the tip of right thumb) are used to designate quantity. *Big* (hold out hands before face then spread them as though giving dimensions) is likewise used to indicate approximate size or quantity. Note that these signs involve no more than one gesture to make them. This becomes an important factor when one attempts to create more complex signs, particularly the compound signs which can become quite difficult to understand since so many signs are needed to form them.

Simple signs, the first sub-type of derived signs, include generally no more than three signs nor less than two. Usually, simple signs are composed of basic signs set in particular series. Not as complex as basic signs in terms of the number of elements required, simple signs may be difficult to grasp if not made correctly. Since they are compounded of basic signs, simple signs require an understanding and fluency in the use of basic signs. Examples of this second type of signs include *Blessed Sacrament* (*bread* + *God*), *barn* (*cow* + *house*), *dinner* (*day* + *eat*), *dormitory* (*sleep* + *house*), *forest* (*all* + *wood* + *courtyard*), *grace* (*finish* + *eat* + *pray*), *librarian* (*choir religious* + *charge* + *book*) and others.

Simple signs may be used to signify a variety of items ranging from objects, such as *barn* and *shed* (*cart* + *wood* + *house*) to things of a more abstract nature, such as *confessor* (*choir religious* + *hear* + *faults*) and *infirmarian* (*choir religious* + *charge* + *sick*). It is interesting to note that the authorized and local lists are composed mostly of basic and simple signs, whereas the list of original signs contains nearly all the compound signs.

Compound signs, the second sub-group of derived signs, contain four or more elements and are difficult to use because of this rather large and unwieldy number of elements. As the complexity of the idea or referent increases, so must the signs to express them. Compound signs are likely to be symbolic of abstract ideas. Moreover, the monks find it necessary to alter or modify older signs to form new ones for new things. Since signs with four or more elements are difficult to make and to remember they are short-lived. They are difficult for the receiver of the message as well since he must often guess what the signer is communicating. Some examples bear out this observation. *Babylon* is signed as *old* (*much* + *year*) + *bad* (take hold of the nostrils with right thumb and forefinger) + *talk* (hold tip of right forefinger near mouth then move finger slightly forward) + *secular* (pass side of right thumb down over mouth and chin) + *courtyard* (hold out forefingers of both hands with tips pointing down then move them in opposite directions in semi-circle); this series of signs literally means "the city about which many evils are said." Misunderstandings might result in a completely garbled message. The individual signer's original choice of signs was dependent upon what he associated with that city and not necessarily what the observer does. We find somewhat the same situation with the series of signs used to symbolize *Bethlehem*: *secular* + *courtyard* + *baby* + *God* + *come*, or "the city where Christ was born." *Egypt* is designated by one monk as *dry* (strike the back of the left hand with tip of right forefinger) + *sand* (hold first two fingers of right hand downwards then rub the tip of right thumb against them several times) + *courtyard* + *arrange* (pass both hands up and down over chest several times in unison) + *pyramid* (describe the top of a pyramid with hands as one would do for *house*), "the desert country (*dry* + *sand* + *courtyard*) where the pyramids were built." Another monk signed *Egypt* as *secular* + *courtyard* + *pharoah* + *stay* and a third signed it as *secular* + *courtyard* + *jew* + *work* + *long* + *time*. Each of these signs is the direct result of what these individual monks associated with Egypt. Finally, *Gethsemane* is signified with the following sequence of signs: *vegetable* + *courtyard* + *cross* + *God* + *pray* + *all* + *time*, or "the garden (*vegetable* + *courtyard*) where Christ (*cross* + *God*) prayed for a long time."

The characters of the *Bible* equally exemplify the problem. *Cain*, for example, is signed as *number* + *one* + *little* + *secular* + *kill* + *brother*, or "the first man to kill his brother." *Job* (*old* + *God* + *book* + *secular* + *cry* + *top* + *manure* + *pile*), *Jonah* (*old* + *God* + *book* + *teacher* + *big* + *fish* + *eat*), and *Judas* (*secular* + *take* + *three* + *o* + *white* + *money* + *kill* + *cross* + *God*) are all signed in complex ways. Translated into speech they are: "Old Testament (*old* + *God* + *book*) character (*secular*) who cried (*cry*) atop (*top*) a manure pile (*manure* + *pile*)"; "Old Testament teacher who was eaten by a big fish"; and "man who took thirty pieces of silver (*white* + *money*) that killed Christ."

Certainly, these examples of compound signs illustrate the complexity of such signs. They also illustrate the fact that these forms are strictly "idiolect" forms; that is, they are quite personal, restricted in a sense to individuals and the particular contexts in which they occur. It is probable that if two or three monks were asked to sign any of the examples noted above (as with *Egypt*) the resulting forms would vary considerably from brother to brother because of what they associate with the places or events. This is less true of basic and simple signs that are signed with some consistency.

Nearly all simple and compound signs are formed according to the word-order of spoken English. One may discern at least two elements in simple signs: one which describes and one which is described. Thus, in the sign for *cake* (*sweet* + *bread*), *sweet* is the describing element and *bread* the element described. *Calf* also adheres to this pattern with *baby* as the describing element and *cow* as the element described. Other examples are *barn* (*cow* + *house*); *bathroom* or *toilet* (*shame* + *house*); *beer* (*corn* + *water*); *mouse* (*cheese* + *animal*), among others.

Although these elements generally adhere to the word-order of spoken English with the describing element in initial position followed by the element described in terminal position, there are many exceptions to this pattern. These exceptions might be the results of the authorized French list being rendered into English. A brief glance at the English translation of this list reveals that most of the signs retain the same word-order as in French. *Psalter*, for example is translated in the English list as *book* + *psalm*, whereas in English practice it would be *psalm* + *book*; the former being the French word-order while the latter is English.[96] Another example is *glace* (*eau* + *dur*), which is translated as *ice* (*water* + *hard*) but it is commonly signed as *hard* + *water* at St Joseph's Abbey. Other instances that betray this include: *bird* (*animal* + *wing*); *chapel* (*church* + *small*); *raw* (*fruit* + *green*); and *snuff-box* (*box* + *snuff*).[97] Each of these examples, when used by English-speaking monks, has the elements reversed so that the describing element is in initial position. Thus, we have *bird* as *wing* + *animal*, *chapel* as *small* + *church*, and so on with the rest of the examples.

We have noted only those signs with two elements but simple signs with three elements also adhere to the same pattern, except that in some instances the initial two elements are combined to form the describing element. Thus, the sign for *honey* (bee's butter) combines *sweet* + *wing* to form the describing element, *bee*. *Martyrology* conforms to essentially the same formula: *all* + *saint* (describing element) and *book* (element described).

Although some possible rules for combining signs have been hinted at in the preceeding discussion, it is quite difficult, if not impossible, to formulate

[96] The French edition of the *Usages* lists the sign as "Le signe de *livre* et de *psaume*g US de l'Orde Cisterciens de la Stricte Observance* (Westmalle, 1926), p. 439.

[97] French originals of these signs are as follows: *oiseau* (*bête* + *aile*); *chapelle* (*église* + *petit*); *cru* (*fruit* + *vert*); *tabatière* (*boîte* + *tabac*) as quoted from the *Usages*. of 1926.

any formal rules that may be applied to both simple and derived signs. We have noted some patterns for simple signs but when they are applied to compound signs they break down because of the very personal and arbitrary nature of such signs. Moreover, even some of the elements included in the simple signs may be arbitrarily placed. For example, the basic sign for *secular* may be either in initial or terminal position. Thus, it may be an element describing or one that is described, as in the following examples: *pagan god* (*secular + god*) and *city* (*secular + courtyard*). In both instances cited, *secular* is a describing element that serves to specify the secular and not the monastic world. However, in some examples *secular* may be placed in other positions depending upon what part of speech it is or what function the sign serves in the utterance. *Pharoah*, for example, may be signed as *king + arrange + old + jew + secular + work + hard*, and *Cain* as *number + one + little + secular + kill + brother*. In terms of the sign language, this could lead to some misunderstanding in the mind of the observer of the message in much the same way that it might if the monks were communicating with speech.

Some signs, on the other hand, must be combined in quite specific patterns, otherwise the meaning would be lost or garbled. Authorized signs must be made according to the rules set down in the *Usages*, at least in theory. In practice as noted, they are made according to the word-order of spoken English. In other instances requiring a definite pattern, the monks generally conform to it as best they can. For example, *queen bee* is signed as *lady + king + sweet + wing*, *lady* and *king* combine to form *queen*, *lady* serving to indicate gender, while *sweet + wing* specify *bee*. If these signs were reversed to read *king + lady*, they would mean "king's lady."

ALPHABET AND SYSTEM OF NUMBERS

Although an alphabet and system of numbers have never been officially recognized by the Order, it is interesting to note that both an alphabet and system of numbers are in use at St Joseph's Abbey. Who invented them, exactly when and where, remains a mystery. One may speculate that they were introduced from Europe or from other monasteries but no written records now extant support this guess. Moreover, there are no common elements with the deaf-mute sign language or any other sign languages noted above. As with other of the countless original signs that are invented to fill the gaps in the sign inventory, the finger alphabet and system of numbers discussed here grew out of a need for more efficient communication among the brothers.

When a signer cannot make his message understood to a fellow monk either because he does not know how to make the required signs, or because he is unable to formulate the message with the available signs, frequently he will resort to spelling out the word or the entire message with his fingers. In this way, the monks are similar to the deaf-mutes because they too spell out words and messages when their messages cannot be understood or when there is a deficiency of signs for expressing themselves. Unlike the deaf-mute's sign language, however, which requires but one hand to sign the alphabet, the monks must use two hands to formulate the letters which are manual representations of the graphic forms.

The monks reproduce the written forms of the alphabetic letters in upper case forms. In this instance, there appears to be a double dependence on speech for the sounds these letters represent and their graphic representations. This is, of course, only partially true of the deaf-mute's sign language alphabet which has an independently symbolic representation of characters completely unrelated to the graphic forms of the alphabet. Thus, with the Cistercian sign language alphabet, the sign for *A* (forefinger and middle finger of left hand held down in an inverted V then right forefinger is placed over middle joints of left fingers to form an upper case A) is truely an *A* formed manually with both right and left hands. Some of the letters are formed with both hands, as with the sign for *A*, but in most instances the letters are formed partially with the left hand and then completed with the right hand which is used to describe a part of the letter. The sign for the letter *B*, for example, is made by holding the left forefinger up from the fist, then the right forefinger is used to describe the loops to complete the letter. In some instances the sign is obvious but to ensure comprehension the letter is further described with the right forefinger, as with the letter *V*: the forefinger and middle finger of the left hand are held vertically from a closed fist with the palm forward, then the right forefinger is used to further describe the letter by running it down one finger then up the other on the inside of both fingers. *J* and *L* are formed in much the same way.

Like most manual number systems, the Cistercians use the fingers and hands exclusively. Whole numbers are made with the fingers while fractions are indicated on the knuckles or combinations of numbers and signs. Thus, the numbers *one* (1) through *ten* (10) are indicated with fingers, i.e., right forefinger is *one* (1) and so on to *ten* with all of the fingers held up. As the numbers become larger, one simply holds up a finger to indicate *one* (1) then adds the sign for the rest of the number, as in *twelve* (12): sign for *one* + sign for *two* equals *twelve*. This can be carried out to ninety-nine if so desired. However, there is a sign for *fifty* (50); in fact, there are two signs. In addition, there is a sign for *hundred* (100). To form *one hundred-fifty*, one simply makes the sign for *hundred* (place tip of right forefinger in open mouth but not in contact) then adds the sign for *fifty* (run right forefinger over middle knuckle of extended left forefinger, or make signs for 5 + o). To make *two hundred* to *nine hundred*, one first makes the sign for *two*, *three*, and so on, then the sign for *hundred*. This method is also used with a *thousand*, which has its own sign (hold up left forefinger then place right forefinger directly atop it to form a T). To indicate, for example, *five thousand*, make the sign for *five* then add the sign for *thousand*. *One hundred thousand* may be made by combining the sign for *hundred* then the sign for *thousand* is added to it. The sign for *million* is the same as the letter *M* and one need only prefix a number to specify how many millions.

Fractions present more of a challenge than whole numbers because the knuckles are used. If one does not indicate the correct knuckle, then things may become confused. However, an alternate method may be used. To specify *three-fourths* (3/4), one may simply use this sequence: *three OVER four*, or *four UNDER three*.

This same method is also used for addition, multiplication and subtraction; that is, signs for *plus*, *times*, and *minus* are utilized to indicate the process involved. To add numbers, say *four* (4) and *five* (5), first make the sign for *four* (4) then the sign for *plus* (hold up left forefinger then place right forefinger across it to form a plus sign, the sign for *five* (5), the sign for *equal* (rub two forefingers together) and finally the sign for *nine* (9). To multiply two numbers, execute the same sequence noted above for addition, except add the sign for *times* (form an X with forefingers) in place of the *plus* sign. To subtract two numbers the following sequence is required: signs for *three* (3), *under*, *four* (4), *equal* and *one* (1).

Ordinal numbers are used only occasionally but when they are needed there are some rules to be observed. All of these occur in the list of original signs only. *First* is signed by making the sign for *number*, then the digit *one* and the sign for *before* and finally the signer must point to the objects in succession. *Second* is made by first indicating the sign for *number*, then *two* and then the sign for *after*, then one points to the first object in the series. The other numbers are patterned in the same manner.

However, there is a slight variation on this method when one is attempting to indicate things that are not present. *Adam*, for example, is signed as *number* + *one* + *secular*; that is, the first man. *Eve* is the *number* + *one* + *secular* + *lady*, or the first woman. Both are not set in series and therefore do not require the *before* sign or the *after* sign as discussed above in the section on ordinal numbers set in series. Other examples are: *Jerusalem* (*number + one + jew + secular + courtyard + j*); *Saul* (*number + one + jew + king*); and *St Stephan* (*number + one + red + saint*), and so on with other examples.

SYNTAX

The sign language of the Cistercian monks is, in reality, nothing more than a lexicon of signs that may be strung together to form phrases and sentences. Just how these signs are patterned into meaningful messages is dependent upon the spoken language of the monks and the monastery in which they live. Thus, monks in the United States and in England model the syntax of their silent messages after English, while in France, French syntax is observed. However, this does not necessarily mean that all utterances must follow English or French word-order since the formation of derived signs often forces the signer to invent new structures, as will be discussed later in this section. This simply means that the monks use this language on a "dialect" and "idiolect" level as represented by these invented structures for which there is no formal set of rules.[98]

On the very simplest level of communication, messages are similar to their spoken counterparts; that is, structures employed follow very closely their speech models. However, as the complexity of the message increases, so must the structure used to convey it. This is not the only reason for garbled messages. Thought patterns of individual monks as well as their knowledge of the signs also create problems in signing messages. The contexts in which the messages are conveyed also play a significant role because many messages

[98] It is interesting to note that there is some question about the "universality" of the Cistercian signs; that is, the use of the signs by all monks, no matter in what speech community they live, among themselves. Of the brothers interviewed, about half felt that the signs are not effective for intercommunity communication. The other half believed that the signs, if used according to the official list in the *Usages*, could be an effective medium of communication. However, there is some question about this latter view, since monks from different speech communities tend to use their spoken languages as models for syntax and morphology. Moreover, there is a tendency to make "dialect" forms of official signs with slightly different physical configurations and shortened versions. Local lists available to this writer reveal a definite tendency in this direction. It should be noted, however, that local lists are reflections of "dialect" forms but in no way represent an effort to counteract the official list of signs. Moreover, the local and "useless" sign lists reflect the language as it is used every day, whereas the official sign list is simply a guideline for making signs, just as a dictionary is for speech.

depend upon the context to be meaningful to the receiver of them. Vocabulary is important too because the inventory of signs is sufficiently small to prevent monks from signing in a meaningful manner. Each of these characteristics will be illustrated and discussed in detail in this section.

The simplest structure is that of the subject-verb-complement pattern in which the verb *be* is prominent. This particular structure clearly illustrates the difficulties monks have with demonstratives. Since there are no signs for them in the inventory of signs, the monks must invent them or simply use the forefinger to indicate the place or thing. Also illustrated in this structure is the problem of pronouns which are most difficult to sign. In the examples given below, context is very significant since, with the demonstratives, their referents must be in close proximity to the conversation so that the monks may point to them or indicate in some fashion just to whom they are referring. In addition, there is no sign for the verb *be*, thus creating a very definite gap in the message to be signed. However, the monks do what is necessary; they interpret the message:[99]

(1) This is Father Robert.
(1a) signs of point to person + PRIEST + R
(1b) signs of point to person + RELIGIOUS + R

(2) He is a monk.
(2a) signs of point to person + RELIGIOUS
(2b) signs of point to person + RELIGIOUS

(3) He is smart.
(3a) signs of point to person + SMART
(3b) signs of point to person + *verb* + LIGHT + HEAD
  (literally, 'he has many lights in his head').

Although this is a fairly simple message, there are very significant gaps in the structure, such as the designation of Father Robert who is identified as *priest* or *religious*, plus the letter *r*. One should also note that both of these signers approach the messages in much the same manner and vary only in their versions of message (3). However, even this variation can be interpreted similarly.

[99] For comparative purposes two and, in some instances, three versions of each sentence are included. Each of the (a) versions was signed by the same brother as were each of the (b) and (c) versions respectively.

Given this basic subject-verb-complement pattern, then, one may increase the complexity of the message by adding a descriptive adjective, as in the following example:

(4) He is an American monk.
(4a) signs of point to person + RELIGIOUS + HERE + COURTYARD + U + S + A
(4b) signs of point to person + HERE + COURTYARD + RELIGIOUS

Obviously, the adjective American complicates the message to the point where it becomes nearly obscured. What both signers are attempting to do is circumvent the original message by re-structuring it. Thus, (4a) should be interpreted as "He is a monk from America"; and (4b) should read as "He is a priest from this monastery which is in America." *This* and *from* are implied rather than stated as such.

The following examples also illustrate the same problem with demonstratives, pronouns and adjectives. The signers again attempt to re-construct the message.

(5) These are books.
(5a) signs of ALL + point to the books in series + BOOK
(5b) signs for point to books + ALL + BOOK

(6) They are old books
(6a) signs of ALL + point to books + OLD + BOOK
(6b) signs of point to books + R + OLD + BOOK

In (6b) the signer has invented a sign for *are* by using the letter *r* which is mentally linked with *they* as implied by pointing to the objects. In a variation to these examples, another monk used the sign for *many* to express plurality, while another inserted the sign for *quantity* (*big* + *number*). In either case, the difficulties with number are evident along with the other problems already discussed, including context.

Within this basic structure a negative may be added so that we have the following example:

(7) He is not tall.
(7a) signs of point to person + NO + TALL

This does not express the pronoun but does preserve the basic construction according to English syntax. This pattern is maintained in the following examples with little or no variation:

(8) He is not here.
(8a) signs of name of person + NO + HERE
(8b) signs of name of person + NO + AROUND + HERE + TODAY
(8c) signs of name of person + NO + COME

The signer of (8b) found it easier to qualify his version by adding *around* and *today* for more clarity. All examples designated as (a) and (b) are signed by the same two monks. Usually (b) varies ever so slightly from (a) or any other versions Another example:

(9) We are in the monastery.
(9a) signs of YOU + ME + UNDER + MONK + HOUSE
(9b) signs of YOU + ME + R + HERE + point to room + HOUSE

The pronoun *me* can be interpreted as *I* and therefore the letter *r* in (9b) added to it makes "You and I *are* in the monastery," or "We *are* in the monastery," two perfectly legitimate variants.

Questions present some difficulties to the monks, primarily because of the lack of an interrogative form. Questions must be preceded by a questioning look or, as some prefer to do, a question mark described in the air with the right forefinger. Both function as markers to indicate that a question is to be asked. However, the markers might be added to the end of the utterance, as in (10a), or a monk might simply begin his question with the letter *r*, as in (11a), to designate *are*, and thus a question. These examples of simple questions (verb-subject-complement) illustrate to what length some monks must go to in order to be understood:

(10) Is that the abbot?
(10a) signs of point to person + ABBOT + questioning look
(10b) signs of WHAT + ABBOT

(11) Are you an American?
(11a) signs of questioning look + YOU + R + SECULAR + COURTYARD + U + S + A (literally, "Is your secular courtyard America?")

One obvious observation as regards questions is that even the very simplest question is most difficult to sign. This becomes increasingly clear when information questions are asked. So too with negative questions with the verb-subject-complement structure, which are illustrated here with only two examples:

(12) Aren't we working?
(12a) signs of YOU + I + WORK + NOW + QUESTION MARK
(12b) signs of R + YOU + ME(I) + WORK

(13) Aren't they brothers?
(13a) signs of point to persons + BROTHER
(13b) signs of point to persons + NO + BROTHER

(12b) comes closer to the original sentence than any of the others. The monk stresses the affirmative in order to convey the negative here. This is frequently done but in the opposite manner: the negative is stressed to convey the affirmative. Plurality, or the lack of it, can be noted. However, given the presence of the brothers, then pointing functions as a pronoun (they) in (13a) and (13b). In (12a) and (12b) *we* cannot be expressed without the persons being present during the conversation.

Question words, such as *who, what, where, when, why,* are all the same in the sign language. Monks attempt to circumlocute them by paraphrasing them in signs, such as *what + time* for *when.* The use of these devices is illustrated in part in the following examples, although other uses will be discussed later. The pattern in which these words are represented is question word-verb-complement, or information questions of a rather simple sort:

(14) Who is the president?
(14a) signs of WHO + PRESIDENT
(14b) signs of WHAT + RELIGIOUS + PRESIDENT + AROUND + HERE.

The assumption on the part of both monks is that the noun *president* refers to the president of the monastery and not the president of the republic. The signer of (14b) qualifies *who* by re-phrasing it to *what + monk* and of the two versions this was best understood by other monks to whom these versions were given.

Other question words used in this structure also are dealt with in the same way as with *who. What,* in particular, offers some interesting material for comment since it is not re-phrased or changed in any way. Whenever other question words are required in an utterance, *what* is usually used because it can mean more than just *what* within the context of the sign language. In fact, *what* may mean *who, where* and *when,* so that confusion in messages might be a problem that can be overcome only by paraphrasing. Furthermore, the sign for *what* is a simple turn of the hand or hands in front of the body and one usually accompanies it with a questioning look to emphasize the question:

(15) What is this?
(15a) signs of WHAT + point to object

(16) Where is the city (Worcester)?
(16a) signs of WHERE (WHAT) + SECULAR + COURTYARD + W
(16b) signs of WHERE (WHAT) + ABOUT + SECULAR + W + COURTYARD

(17) When is matins?
(17a) signs of WHAT + TIME + NIGHT + SING
(17b) signs of WHAT + TIME + MORNING + PRAY

Of the three sentences signed to demonstrate the information question pattern, (17a) and (17b) come closest to the original. The question word, *where*, tends to confuse (16) and its versions. (16b) attempts to re-phrase *where* with little success. And, of course, there is the problem of a sign for the city of Worcester which must be signed as *secular + courtyard + W* or *secular + W + courtyard*. Either way the designation is tenuous at best if one is not familiar with the city and the fact that it is located near the Abbey.

This subject-verb-complement pattern is further illustrated by adding describing words (adjectives) to the examples. Note the lack of articles and the substitution of the sign *here* for *this*, another instance in which context plays an important role:

(18) This room is large.
(18a) signs of THIS (HERE) + HOUSE + MUCH + BIG
(18b) signs of THIS (HERE) + ROOM + BIG

(19) This room is light.
(19a) signs of THIS (HERE) + MUCH + LIGHT + UNDER + HOUSE
(19b) signs of THIS (HERE) + LIGHT + UNDER + ROOM.

Of interest in (19) is the lack of the sign for *in* which is implied in the literal translation of the sentence from the signs: "There is much light in this room," or "This room is very light." In versions (18a) and (19a), the signs for *house* and *room* are used interchangeably with little loss of meaning, although the basic structure is still preserved to some extent.

However, this is not true of the following example which has the same basic structure as (18) and (19), but it is slightly varied to accommodate the lengthy subject and complement. Both are designated not by their signs but rather by what job the subject performs (Brother Pascal) and, for American, the paraphrasing, *courtyard* + U + S + A and *this (here)* + *side* + *water*:

(20) Brother Pascal is American.
(20a) signs of BROTHER + CHARGE + SECULAR + HOUSE + COME + THIS (HERE) + SIDE + WATER
(20b) signs of BROTHER + CHARGE + SECULAR + HOUSE + COME + THIS (HERE) COURTYARD + U + S + A.

Read literally, (20a) is "The brother in charge of the guest house is from this side of the ocean." Version (20b) may be read as "The brother in charge of the guest house is from America." Since Brother is the *guest master*, he is identified by his position and not by name. This is done quite frequently, as the list of St Joseph's members reveals.

Motion verbs are also illustrated in the subject-verb-complement pattern. However, as with some of the verbs, there are no specific signs for them so the monks must call upon their ingenuity to either invent signs on the spur of the moment or resort to circumlocution. In these particular examples *quick*, if in the final position, may mean *early* rather than indicate speed:

(21) The monk hurries to work.
(21a) signs of RELIGIOUS + GO + WORK + QUICK
(21b) signs of RELIGIOUS + GO + QUICK + TWO + WORK

(22) The monk goes home.
(22a) signs of RELIGIOUS + GO + SECULAR + HOME
(22b) signs of RELIGIOUS + GO + BACK + HOUSE (HOME)

(23) The boy rides home.
(23a) signs of LITTLE + SECULAR + BULL + DRIVE + HOME
(23b) signs of LITTLE + SECULAR + DRIVE + BACK + HOME.

Examples (22a) and (22b) are interesting because both monks assume that the word *home* must mean *secular home* and not the monastery; (23a) and (23b) also preserve this form by implication since no children live in the monastery. This is further supported by the signs of *boy* which presume a *secular* child. Of interest also is the designation for masculine gender, *little + secular + bull*, the latter sign indicating masculinity.

In a number of examples not noted here, the sign for *go* is substituted for motion verbs as *travel, run,* and *fly*, although the latter does have its own sign. One version repeats two motion verbs to emphasize speed but generally the basic meanings are intended. One example is offered here:

(24) The farmer runs to work.
(24a) signs of SECULAR + CHARGE + HAY + COURTYARD + GO + TWO + WORK + RUN
(24b) signs of SECULAR + CHARGE + VEGETABLE + COURTYARD + RUN + TWO + WORK.

When a verb has its own sign, that is, one specified in the lists, it is very unlikely that the basic structure of a sentence will be altered significantly. Verbs, such as *walk* and *go*, are positioned according to English word order in these examples:

(25) He walks to the barn.
(25a) signs of SECULAR + WALK + TWO + COW + HOUSE
(25b) signs of SECULAR + WALK + COW + HOUSE

(26) He goes to the fields.
(26a) signs of SECULAR + GO + TWO + HAY + COURTYARD
(26b) signs of SECULAR + GO + TWO + VEGETABLE + COURTYARD.

The basic structure of the subject-verb-object with place and/or time phrases or words added is essentially the same in the examples noted below, although there is a bit of confusion as the result of compound signs. In examples (27a) and (27b) the subject is identified only by what position he holds within the self-governing body. However, to the monks such a designation would be easily understood since they are aware of this:

(27) Father Robert lives in a cell.
(27a) signs of SUB-PRIOR + STAY + UNDER + LITTLE + PRIVATE + HOUSE + ALL + TIME
(27b) signs of SUB-PRIOR + HIDE + UNDER + SLEEP + HOUSE

(28) John eats dinner at 7:30 in the evening.
(28a) signs of J + EAT + DAY + EAT + HALF + AFTER + SEVEN + NIGHT + TIME

(28b) signs of SECULAR + J + EAT + DAY + EAT + HALF + AFTER + SEVEN +
       NIGHT + TIME

 (29) They read in the library every afternoon.
(29a) signs of ALL + point to persons present + READ + UNDER + BOOK +
       HOUSE + EVERY + DAY + AFTER + EAT
(29b) signs of ALL + RELIGIOUS + READ + UNDER + BOOK + HOUSE + ALL +
       AFTER + DAY + EAT.

All examples retain a recognizable pattern similar to the original sentences.
(27a) has a phrase added on for emphasis (*all* + *time*) while (27b) uses the sign
for *dormitory* (*sleep* + *house*) and not that of *cell* (*little* + *private* + *house*).
(28b) varies from (28a) only in the initial sign which, in (28b) assumes a
secular and not a *religious* because the brothers do not eat that late in the
evening. To express plurality or number (29a) and (29b) add the sign for all
at the very beginning of each version and (29b) uses the sign for *all* a second
time to express *every* before *afternoon* (*after* + *day* + *eat*).

The negative, in all the examples presented thus far, is placed in the
position one would find in speech patterns. Thus, in the subject-verb-complement pattern, *no* and *not* are positioned correctly, at least in terms of speech:

 (30) The monk does not eat.
(30a) signs of BROTHER + NO + EAT
(30b) signs of RELIGIOUS + NO + EAT + NOW

The pattern is basically the same in the other examples already noted, (7)
and (8), and also in the subject-verb-object pattern. *Do* forms are also omitted.

Question words used in this subject-verb-object with time and/or place
phrases or words, such as *who*, present no difficulty to the monks. *Who*, in
the examples noted below, is re-phrased to *what* + *religious* but even this
alteration is kept within the basic pattern:

 (31) Who lives in a small cell?
(31a) signs of WHAT + RELIGIOUS + HIDE + UNDER + LITTLE + PRIVATE +
       HOUSE
(31b) signs of question mark + WHAT + RELIGIOUS + STAY + UNDER +
       LITTLE + PRIVATE + HOUSE

 (32) Who studies on Saturdays in the library?
(32a) signs of WHAT + RELIGIOUS + WORK + BOOK + MOTHER + GOD + DAY
       + UNDER + BOOK + HOUSE

(32b) signs of question mark + WHAT + RELIGIOUS + THINK + BOOK + MOTHER + GOD + DAY + UNDER + BOOK + HOUSE.

Versions (31a) and (31b) each use different verbs in place of the original verb, *lives*, which is significant, at least for the brothers within the community. *Stay* implies permanency while *hide* simply means to live within a place over a period of time. (31b) and (32b) are both signed by the same monk and it is curious to observe that this particular monk includes a question mark before each version to ensure understanding on the part of the observer. (32b) also alters the text by using *think* to mean *mull over* rather than *to study*, yet throughout maintaining the basic structure of the pattern.

Another basic pattern of English is the subject-verb-phrase-object and place phrase or word added to the end. The problem which looms largest here is the sign for the verb *ask*, which does not exist in the inventory of either authorized or original signs. Thus, substitutes, sometimes inappropriate, are invented to fill the gap. (33) was signed in a number of different ways each with different verbs but somehow each was understood by other monks to whom the examples were given for comment. Number is always a problem in the Cistercian sign language, as noted earlier, and the examples offered here support this, particularly with collective nouns like *people*. The sign for *many*, or *much*, is often used to express or indicate plurality:

(33) A tall monk is asking a question.
(33a) signs of TALL + RELIGIOUS + GIVE + MANY + LITTLE + question mark signed several times
(33b) signs of ONE + TALL + RELIGIOUS + ARRANGE + question mark signed several times

(34) Many people are eating in the refectory.
(34a) signs of RIGHT + NOW + MANY + RELIGIOUS + EAT + DOWN + IN + EAT + HOUSE
(34b) signs of RIGHT + NOW + EAT + HOUSE + FILL + RELIGIOUS

(35) One student is looking up a word in the dictionary.
(35a) signs of ONE + RELIGIOUS + GO + TWO + BOOK + CHAPTER + GO + TWO + LOOK + UP + WRITE + UNDER + BOOK
(35b) signs of ONE + RELIGIOUS + WHO + GO + TWO + BOOK + CHAPTER + TWO + LOOK + UP + WRITE + UNDER + BOOK

Of the examples given here, (35a) and (35b) are most representative of what might happen when a brother is called upon to invent signs for vocabulary that does not exist. *Student,* for instance, does not have an authorized sign but rather many original signs which are not understood by all of the members of the monastery. Thus, in both examples, the signers invented appropriate signs to indicate *student* but only in terms of the monastic life can the signs used in combination be fully comprehended. Translated literally, (35a) means "One of the monks who attends classes (*one + religious + go + two + book + chapter*) goes to look up a word (*write*) in a book." There is no specific reference to a dictionary but by implication the signs, *write + under + book,* means dictionary.

In versions (33a) and (33b), the signs for *asking* are *give* and *arrange* but in other versions of this same sentence signs for *make* and *raise* were also used. In addition, the difficulty of signing *question* in this context is nearly insurmountable to both the brothers and they simply repeated the question mark several times to designate plurality. The result is, of course, a garbled message which to most is not easily understood.

The interrogative forms of the preceding structure present many of the problems noted above. Monks, for example, do not invent signs for *is*; thus the initial element is omitted as is the sign for *asking,* for which *give* and *speak* are substituted:

(36) Is the old monk asking a question?
(36a) signs of OLD + RELIGIOUS + YOU + KNOW + GIVE + QUESTION (mark)
(36b) signs of OLD + RELIGIOUS + YOU + KNOW + SPEAK + QUESTION (mark)

(37) Is the young monk asking a question?
(37a) signs of CHILD + BABY + RELIGIOUS + YOU + KNOW + GIVE + QUESTION (mark)

(38) Are they praying in church?
(38a) signs of ALL + RELIGIOUS + PRAY + UNDER + CHURCH + question mark
(38b) signs of YOU + THINK + ALL + RELIGIOUS + PRAY + UNDER + CHURCH

Examples (36a) and (36b) both do not have signs for *question,* and since the sign for *question* in some contexts can be a simple question mark drawn in the air at the end of a sentence or after it, the problem in both of these versions arises from the position of *question* in the original sentence. One might interpret the versions as meaning a statement such as "The old monk is asking a question," rather than the interrogative form; the question mark at the end could indicate a noun or it could indicate a question mark. The viewer might not perceive the difference quickly. The same comment applies to (37a).

The question word-verb phrase-object-place pattern offers little trouble to the monks. A question mark at the end of each sentence is not required since the question word suffices:

(39) Who is working in the fields?
(39a) signs of WHAT + RELIGIOUS + WORK + HAY + COURTYARD + NOW
(39b) signs of WHAT + RELIGIOUS + WORK + NOW + HAY + COURTYARD

(40) Who is studying English in the library?
(40a) signs of WHO (WHAT + RELIGIOUS) + WORK + BOOK + ABOUT + E + TONGUE + NOW + UNDER + BOOK + HOUSE
(40b) signs of WHO (WHAT + RELIGIOUS) + WORK + OVER + E + TONGUE + UNDER + BOOK + HOUSE + NOW

(41) What are many monks doing?
(41a) signs of WHAT + R + MANY + RELIGIOUS + UP + TWO
(41b) signs of WHAT + MANY + RELIGIOUS + ARRANGE + NOW

There, when placed in the subject position in a pattern, cannot be expressed nor can the form of *be* following it. When linked with a collective noun such as *group*, the pattern becomes garbled to a great extent as in the examples:

(42) There is a large group in the church.
(42a) signs of RIGHT + NOW + CHURCH + FILL
(42b) signs of RIGHT + NOW + CHURCH + STAY + BIG + NUMBER + LOAD + SECULAR

(43) There are many books in the room.
(43a) signs of HOUSE + FILL + BOOK
(43b) signs of MANY + BOOK + UNDER + ROOM

Both subject and verb are completely omitted leaving the receiver of the message to interpret the message. Obviously, the signs expressing *large group* in (42b) become quite arbitrary.

Another pattern that presents some difficulty to the signers is the question word-verb *(be)*- there-subject-place or time pattern. As in the examples noted in (42) and (43), *there* and the form of *be* are implied rather than stated specifically. Thus, the viewer must once again interpret the message rather than receive it directly:

(44) When are the people in the library?

(44a) signs of WHAT + TIME + SECULAR + COME + TWO + BOOK + HOUSE
(44b) signs of WHAT + TIME + RELIGIOUS + GO + TWO + BOOK + HOUSE

(45) Where are the many people at noon?
(45a) signs of WHERE (WHAT) + ABOUT + MANY + SECULAR + HIDE + EAT + TIME
(45b) signs of DAY + EAT + TIME + WHAT + TIME + ALL + RELIGIOUS + HIDE

Example (45a) substitutes the sign *about* for *are* in an attempt to compensate for the lack of a sign for any form of *be*. The time phrase *at noon* is made to coincide with the signs for *lunch* in (45a) to express that time of day. Structurally, the examples are acceptable, except (45b) which is quite unacceptable because it is not a question but rather a statement. The question word *what* is obviously misplaced in this version. Had it been placed in initial position the structure would have been maintained.

Time and place expressions generally present some difficulty to the monks who use the signs, especially when they are placed in initial position in a sentence. There is a tendency for the signer to move such expressions to another position which essentially means that they are altering the pattern to one they are able to use easily:

(46) At eight o'clock the priest goes to work.
(46a) signs of SECULAR + PRIEST (RELIGIOUS) + GO + TWO + WORK + 8 + O + A + M + WRITE + ON + NOSE
(46b) signs of RELIGIOUS + GO + WORK + 8 + MORNING

(47) In the afternoon he studies literature.
(47a) signs of AFTER + DAY + EAT + WORK + TONGUE + RULE
(47b) signs of AFTER + DAY + EAT + WORK + BOOK + ABOUT + E + TONGUE + RULE

(48) In the refectory we eat every noon.
(48a) signs of ALL + DAY + EAT + DAY + EAT + UNDER + EAT + HOUSE
(48b) signs of EVERY + DAY + EAT + DAY + EAT + HIGH + NOON + ONE + + TWO

O, in (46a), is used to mean *o'clock* but the signer felt it necessary to further qualify the time by adding the phrase, *write + on + nose* (literally, "right on the nose," or exactly). (48a) and (48b) both express *every noon* with similar signs: (48a) *all + day* and (48b) *every + day* but the expression of *noon* is lost as a result in (48a). However, this is made up for by the inclusion of *day + eat* (*noon meal*), but one must remain alert to the different compound signs in which *eat* occurs. There is a tendency on the part of the viewer to group all these signs together as one long one or interpret one to belong to the preceding one, as in (48a) *all + day* (*every day*); *all + day + eat* (*every noon meal*) and so on.

Adverbs of frequency, such as *usually, rarely,* and *frequently,* are ingeniously circumlocuted with other signs. Unfortunately, the exact meanings of these adverbs are somewhat more vague or general when this is done. Nevertheless, the essential meanings do come through so that one is able to grasp what the signer is trying to convey. The position of these adverbs adheres quite closely to their position in speech patterns; at least, this is true of the examples noted below:

(49) The monk usually goes to church at 8 o'clock.

(49a) signs of RELIGIOUS + CLOSE + TWO + ALL + TIME + GO + TWO + CHURCH + 8 + O (O'CLOCK)

(49b) signs of MANY + TIME + RELIGIOUS + GO + TWO + CHURCH + 8 + O'CLOCK

(50) Rarely does the monk pray in church.

(50a) signs of NOT + TWO + MANY + TIME + RELIGIOUS + PRAY + UNDER + CHURCH

(50b) signs of RELIGIOUS + NO + PRAY + TWO + MANY + TIME + UNDER + CHURCH

Usually, as expressed in (49a), is *close + two + all + time,* which can be said to be nearly all the time; in other words, the monk can be found at 8 o'clock in church most of the time. However, in (49b) *usually* is expressed in the signs *many + time* which is not quite the same as *usually.* (50a) and (50b) express *rarely* much like speech even including the negative to further emphasize frequency.

Frequency, as expressed in (51a) and (51b), is the same as *usually* (*many + time*):

(51) The choir is frequently in church at night.

(51a) signs of ALL + SING + RELIGIOUS + MANY + TIME + UNDER + CHURCH + NIGHT + TIME

(51b) signs of ALL + SING + RELIGIOUS + MUCH + TIME + UNDER + CHURCH + EVENING

There is every indication that this pattern is maintained as regards adverbs of frequency and their position in sentence patterns of any type. Such is basically true of the negative which is most often placed after the adverb, as in this example:

(52) The choir is not frequently in church at night.
(52a) signs of ALL + SING + RELIGIOUS + MANY + TIME + NOT + UNDER + CHURCH + NIGHT

which, when literally translated means "The choir is frequently not in church at night." Thus, the negative is placed after the adverb of frequency rather than before it as in the original sentence.

Dependent clauses, when added to basic sentence-patterns, are quite difficult to express in the Cistercian sign language. However, the shorter the clause the less difficult it is to express. As the clause increases in complexity the greater the task of the signer to express it in intelligible signs. The addition of such clauses is one source of garbling in the language and most, if not all, the monks interviewed had some trouble with them. The examples, although quite simple, illustrate the problem:

(53) I just bought a house in the town where he is living.
(53a) signs of I (ME) + FINISH + BUY + ONE + HOUSE + CLOSE + SECULAR + COURTYARD + CLOSE + TWO + ME + FRIEND + SECULAR + HOUSE
(53b) signs of I (ME) + JUST + BUY + HOUSE + NEXT + TWO + ME + FRIEND + SECULAR + COURTYARD + HOUSE

(53a) is an attempt to express tense (*finish* + *buy*) but it must be implied only because the sign language cannot express anything more complex than present or simple past. The indefinite article *a* is designated as *one* but the rest of the sentence is quite difficult to express. The phrase *in the town* comes through as *close* + *two* + *secular* + *courtyard*, *close* + *two* meaning *in* within the context of these signs. The dependent clause *where he is living* becomes *close* + *two* + *me* + *friend* + *secular* + *house*. The possessive is expressed here which was not even inferred in the original statement. In addition, the signer of (53a) specifies *secular* + *house*, the secular world being implied in the whole sentence. But more significantly, the verb *living* is omitted altogether.

(53b) is signed somewhat differently. An interpretation of the version is: "I just bought a house next to my secular friend's city (town) house." *Just* seems to express the fact that the transaction took place within a very recent period of time, although this is not completely clear. Again there is an attempt to express the possessive with the signs *me + friend* (my friend's). The dependent clause in both (53a) and (53b) is completely lost.

An excellent example of what happens to a sentence when it is translated into the sign language is the following:

(54) We all eat when Jack's parents come to visit.
(54a) signs of TIME + SECULAR + JACK + COME + ALL + EAT + EQUAL + TIME + point to + SECULAR + MOTHER + FATHER + COME

The dependent clause becomes garbled and unintelligible. A more detailed analysis reveals that elements in the original sentence cannot be related to each other. When translated back into English speech, the version reads about as follows: "When (as expressed by *time*) Jack comes we (*all*) eat like the time his (as expressed by *point to*) mother and father come." There is no possessive nor is there even a basic sentence pattern, as in the original sentence. Other versions of (54) are as garbled as (54a).

Another example of a fairly lengthy basic sentence pattern with a short dependent clause is (55). Actually, the version offered here is representative of how the monks signed it with little variation, except for the word order and diction of the clause. It is quite readily understood with little interpretation required by the viewer. However, (55a) does express the connective *but* (*all + same*) which other versions not presented failed to do:

(55) The monks know how to plant vegetables but we don't.
(55a) signs of ALL + RELIGIOUS (MONK) + KNOW + RULE + TWO + GIVE + VEGETABLE + SEED + ALL + SAME + YOU + ME + NOT + KNOW + RULE

A variation of the last segment of the sentence following *but* (*all + same*) is *you + me + not + know + four + arrange*. Implied in this utterance is ". . . we do not know how to plant," which echoes the signs for *plant* in the preceding segment, which are *give + vegetable + seed*.

Many of the monks, when asked to sign the following example, interpreted the sentence in much the same way. But there is no sign for *harvest* or the verb form *harvesting*, thus the signers called upon their imagination and responded as in this example:

(56) The fields are ready for harvesting but the orchards are not.
(56a) signs of CLOSE + TWO + TIME + MOW + HAY + NOW + ALL + SAME + NOT + CLOSE + TWO + TIME + TWO + PICK + FRUIT

Translated into speech the signs mean "It is close to the time to mow the hay but it is not time to pick the fruit." The basic meaning of the original sentence is retained in this and other versions but the circuitous route the monks took seemed to confuse many of the brothers asked to comment upon the versions. Nonetheless, as with other sentences and their signed versions, some of the brothers grasped immediately the meaning with little hesitation.

If clauses expressing the conditional are not easily interpreted and signed by the monks. Since there is no sign for *if* one must simply preface the statement with a questioning look on one's face, which can cause some trouble for the viewer. Moreover, if the conditional clause is in initial position in the statement then one must be careful to see that the viewer notes the puzzled look, otherwise the message could become garbled in the interpretation. The result clause offers little difficulty if signed with care:

(57) If you come tonight we will go to the restaurant.

(57a) signs of TIME + YOU + COME + THIS (NOW) + NIGHT + ALL + GO + TWO + EAT + HOUSE

(57b) signs of AFTER + YOU + ARRANGE + YOU + HEAD + TWO + COME + THIS (NOW) + NIGHT + YOU + ME + GO + TWO + SECULAR + EAT + HOUSE

Time in (57a) when linked with a puzzled look on the face means *if* or *when*. The latter possibility rules out the conditional altogether. (57b), on the other hand, uses *after* to express *if* but it too can mean something else. In fact, the segment following *after* (*you* + *arrange* + *you* + *head*) means "after you decide to come," rather than "if you come tonight."

Other examples of if-clauses reveal the difficulty the brothers have with the conditional

(58) If I had a good job I could live in luxury.

(58a) signs of TIME + I + TAKE + GOOD + WORK + I + TAKE + MUCH + SOFT

(58b) signs of GIVE + ME + GOOD + WORK + I + B + EQUAL + KING

Time, as in previously noted if-clauses can mean *if* but it must be linked with a puzzled look on the face of the signer or its meaning becomes unintelligible.

Future conditional, as with the other conditionals, cannot be expressed. Therefore, both the result and conditional clauses present some obvious problems to the monks. Questions, in particular, are of interest here because they seem to be representative examples of these problems:

(59) What will you do if you don't take the exam?
(59a) signs of TIME + YOU + NOT + TAKE + X + PAPER + WHAT + YOU + ARRANGE
(59b) signs of WHAT + YOU + ARRANGE + NOT + TAKE + X + PAPER

The signer of (59a) has reversed the structure by placing the if-clause first then the question, although the version is not difficult to understand. (59b) retains the basic pattern of the original but it leaves out the if-clause but it is there by implication. Significantly, both signers leave out the question mark sign and thereby rely upon the question word *what* to indicate a question.

Like the previously discussed if-clauses (conditional clauses), reason clauses are troublesome to the monks. They are rarely used because there is no way to express the connective *because*. (60a) illustrates this point:

(60) I took my small suitcase because my large one was broken.
(60a) signs of I + TAKE + ME + SMALL + SUITCASE + ME + LARGE + ONE + BREAK

(60b) signs of I + CARRY + SMALL + SUITCASE + LARGE + SUITCASE + BREAK

The obvious need is for a connection in both versions to establish the relationship between the two clauses.

Monks do not differentiate between restrictive and non-restrictive clauses. They simply look at a sentence and then interpret it. Only after this do they attempt to sign their interpretation. Clauses are generally not considered important, as the following examples illustrate. Note that *which* and *who* are omitted but in (61a) the sense still comes through clearly. However, this is not the case with (62a) and (62b) which leave out the *who* but do attempt to state it.

(61) The book which we are studying is very difficult.
(61a) signs of BOOK + YOU + ME + WORK + OVER + MUCH + HARD
(61b) signs of YOU + ME + WORK + OVER + MUCH + HARD + BOOK

(62) George's brother, who has a car, went to Boston.
(62a) signs of G + SECULAR + RED + WATER + BROTHER + ONE + DRIVE + MACHINE + GO + TWO + B + COURTYARD
(62b) signs of BROTHER + TWO + G + SAME + ONE + TAKE + MACHINE + GO + TWO + B + T (TOWN)

Of the two sentences, it is the latter one (62) that causes the greatest confusion. This might be the result of the possessive combined with the clause. The clause in both versions is introduced by *one* or *same + one*, and *who* is implied.

Sentence patterns that express comparisons are used to only a very limited extent. Degrees of sameness can be expressed with some preciseness depending upon the sentence and its structure. *Alike, like,* and *the same as* are all designated by the signs for *equal* or *about*, without regard for degree of similarity. Note also that *equal* and *same* have the same sign and don't really vary too much in meaning:

(63) He is the same age as John.
(63a) point to person + SAME + OLD + LIKE + J
(63b) signs of SECULAR + EQUAL + YEAR + LIKE + J

(64) My car is the same color as yours.
(64a) signs of ME + DRIVE + MACHINE + SAME + PAINT + LIKE + YOU + DRIVE + MACHINE
(64b) signs of PAINT + ME + DRIVE + MACHINE + EQUAL + TWO + YOU + DRIVE + MACHINE

(65) Your pen and mine are alike.
(65a) signs of YOU + ME + WRITE + TOOL + EQUAL

(66) The two chairs in this room are alike.
(66a) signs of TWO + LITTLE + WOOD + EQUAL
(66b) signs of TWO + LITTLE + WOOD + SAME + UNDER + HOUSE

(67) Your book is like mine.
(67a) signs of YOU + ME + BOOK + SAME
(67b) signs of YOU + ME + BOOK + CLOSE + TWO + SAME

(63a) and (63b) express *same* in slightly different ways, although the signs are alike. (63a) implies an approximation of age (middle age, and so on), whereas (63b) is quite precise. (64a) and (64b) express the similarity of color in the same manner as do (65a), (66a) and (66b). However, the signer of (67a) and the signer of (67b) alter this pattern by attempting to express degrees of similarity. (67a) indicates an exact similarity whereas (67b) indicates only a degree of sameness when he uses the signs CLOSE + TWO + SAME. Some examples not offered here use the signs of *equal + good + like* to express *as well as* and the signs of *sew + hard* to designate *as hard as*, each an attempt to express a degree of sameness.

Degrees of comparison can be made with some logic. However, the examples offered here were signed apart from any context. When the comparative

is used in the context of a sentence, the degree to which the items are compared is often lost as the result of the patterning of the message. The adjectives
compared here have been categorized according to traditional grammar
but once again, as with so much of the Cistercian sign language, context is
important. For example, the choice of *much* or *more* to form the comparative
degree will depend upon the signer and his peculiar habits of signing and
upon the adjective or adverb, whichever the case might be.

There is a very definite pattern which can be observed when the three
degrees are formed, as the table illustrates.

	COMPARISON	
POSITIVE	**COMPARATIVE**	**SUPERLATIVE**
young	**younger**	**youngest**
sign of CHILD or BABY	signs of MORE + CHILD	signs of # + ONE + CHILD
old	**older**	**oldest**
signs of OLD	signs of MORE + OLD	signs of # + ONE + OLD
lively	**livelier**	**liveliest**
signs of MUCH + WILD	signs of MORE + WILD	signs of # + ONE + WILD
serious	**more serious**	**most serious**
signs of WORRY + OVER	signs of COME + MORE + WORRY	signs of # + ONE + WORRY + OVER
pretty	**prettier**	**prettiest**
signs of PRETTY	signs of MORE + PRETTY	signs of # + ONE + PRETTY
good	**better**	**best**
sign of GOOD	signs of MORE + GOOD	signs of # + ONE + GOOD
bad	**worse**	**worst**
sign of BAD	signs of MORE + BAD	signs of # + ONE + BAD
little	**less** (than)	**least**
sign of LITTLE	signs of MORE + LITTLE	signs of # + ONE + LITTLE + UNDER + ALL

TABLE ONE—the sign for **more** is simply made with **much** but the sign is
repeated several times. **Most** is expressed by the signs # + **one**, as in the
superlative.

A most perplexing feature of the Cistercian sign language is its lack of tense and verb forms, other than the simple. One can appreciate the complexity of attempting to indicate the past, future or present with any accuracy without such features. In such instances requiring a designation of time, most of the brothers add qualifying signs or phrases to convey tense. But even with these devices the problem seems insurmountable because the nuances of time and action are lost in a maze of signs which seem to indicate tense but which are not accurate enough to be of real value.

Nonetheless, most of the monks who use the sign language imaginatively are able to indicate tenses to some degree. Simple future and simple past are signed with a wave of the right fist, palm forward, out from the right shoulder (future) and a wave of the right fist back over the right shoulder (past) To indicate a greater time, then, the signs are repeated several times. Such signs are inadequate for exact expressions of duration of time To compensate for this inadequacy, the signers usually add more signs to try to express time, which might be considered a defect in the language and certainly a complicating factor. In this regard, one might further observe that some signers attempt to be too accurate and thus add more and more signs until the meaning of the sentence is lost.

In all instances in which tense must be expressed, the simple form of the verb is used. Frequently, the infinitive must be expressed and in such situations the monks can add the sign for *two* before signing the simple form of the verb, as in the following example:

(68) I want you to come to the city.
(68a) signs of I + LIKE + YOU +   COME + SECULAR + COURTYARD
(68b) signs of I + LIKE + YOU + TWO + COME + TWO + SECULAR + COURTYARD

The *two* in (68b) is not necessary but the signer included it for clarity.

A particularly interesting feature of the sign language is the lack of the verb *be* either in simple form or otherwise. However, the signers have invented means for expressing its forms in the present tense The first person singular present is signed as *m*, as in *I* + *m* (I'm), or the plural form *r*, as in *you* + *me* + *r* (we're), or *you* + *r* (you're). (69) illustrates this:

(69) We are here.
(69a) signs of YOU + ME + R + HERE

If the singular and plural present forms are not signed in this manner then they must be inferred from the context in which they are silently noted.

Have presents some difficulty to the monks since there is no designated sign for the verb. However, *have* can be expressed by the use of the sign for the verb *take*. The use of this sign for expressing *have* might create some confusion, so the signer must be very certain of the context before employing it. In fact, the signer should be certain that the viewer understands the context, otherwise garbling will result. The example which follows is taken from a dialogue but its meaning must be considered carefully since it is lifted from a context:

(70) I have a book.
(70a) signs of I + TAKE + ONE + BOOK

The obvious ambiguity of the sentence is clear. Auxiliary verbs cannot be employed with any real accuracy, although the more ingenious monks somehow include a sign or two to express them if possible.

Unlike the present tense, the simple past is quite difficult for the signers because of the lack of verb forms. A simple sentence like

(71) The book was open.
can be altered to fit the past by adding the sign for *before*, as in
(71a) signs of BEFORE + BOOK + OPEN.

Another example employs a different phrase to express past tense but its use implies that the event took place further back in time:

(72) I went to Boston.
(72a) signs of LONG + TIME + BACK + I + GO + TWO + B + COURTYARD

In another version of (72), the signer used *before* rather than *long + time + back*.

All of the perfect tenses, particularly the present perfect and past perfect, are most awkward for the monks to sign. The same expressions used in the simple past are often employed:

(73) The book has been open for some time.
(73a) signs of point to + BOOK + OPEN + LONG + TIME + NOW
(73b) signs of point to + BOOK + SEPARATE + NOW + FOUR + LONG + TIME

The signer of (73a) places *now*, to link the actions to the present at the end of the sentence and does not use *four*, as does the signer of (73b). The phrase *four + long + time* gives the viewer some indication that the action took place in the past and is continuing, whereas (73a) uses *long + time* but this does not seem to express the same sense, although it does indicate that the action did take place in the past.

The past perfect tense is expressed in much the same fashion as the present perfect. However, most signers add the sign for *before* in initial position in the sentence and *four + long + time* at the end to better designate a completed action in the past:

(74) The book had been open for a long time.
(74a) signs of BEFORE + point to + BOOK + SEPARATE + FOUR + LONG + TIME
(74b) signs of BEFORE + point to + BOOK + SEPARATE + FOUR + A + LONG + TIME

The signer of (74b) added the sign for *a* to conform to a speech pattern but in no way altered the meaning of the sentence.

As discussed earlier, the simple future is expressed by a simple wave of the right fist forward before the right shoulder; this sign means *before* or *tomorrow*. When used in a sentence expressing the future the sign can mean *next*, as in

(75) I'll see you next week.
(75a) signs of I + SEE + YOU + NEXT + WEEK

Next + week indicates that the event will take place in one week. The burden of expressing the future is carried by this phrase since no verb form is used. If the signer wished to indicate a greater time in the future, then the sign for *next* would be made twice or perhaps repeated several times.

There are other ways of expressing the simple future which are more accurate and easily understood. However, these methods do not include the use of *shall* or *will* but rather other verb forms such as *going to*, which can be used to express future time:

(76) I am going to invite you to supper next week.
(76a) signs of I + ASK + YOU + TWO + NIGHT + EAT + NEXT + WEEK

(77) I will show you when she comes.
(77a) signs of TIME + SHE (sign name of person) + COME + I + SHOW + YOU + ALL + ABOUT + GIVE + RULE

Time is used to imply *when* in (77a). The exact time when she will arrive is not clearly stated even in the original sentence, so the signer of (81a) is equally vague with the expression of time.

Question patterns involving the simple future exhibit somewhat the same characteristics as the statement patterns. Basic structures are maintained wherever and whenever possible:

(78) Who is going to have dinner next week?
(78a) signs of WHAT + SECULAR + ARRANGE + DAY + EAT + NEXT + WEEK

(79) What will you do when your mother arrives?
(79a) signs of TIME + YOU + SECULAR + MOTHER + ARRIVE + WHAT + YOU + ARRANGE

(80) Where will you eat tonight?
(80a) signs of WHEN + ABOUT + YOU + EAT + NOW (THIS) + NIGHT
(80b) signs of WHAT + SECULAR + COURTYARD + YOU + EAT + THIS + NIGHT

Time, as in (77a) is used in (79a) to express *when*. Thus, (79a) might be translated as "When your mother arrives what will you have planned?" The other examples are altered in their versions but nonetheless the basic meanings come through quite clearly with little confusion.

It is possible to use a negative phrase to further express future time. The negative plus the sign for *now* emphasize the future, as in this example:

(81) I will receive some paints next week.
(81a) signs of I + TAKE + PAINT + NEXT + WEEK + NOT + NOW

To express the future perfect tense, the brothers utilize any number of invented signs. However, one can express some action that will be completed at some point between the present and a future time; that is, if one is ingenious enough to exploit the limited possibilities available. Perhaps (82a) and (82b) will make this point clear:

(82) I will have gone to the movies by next week.
(82a) signs of NOW (THIS) + TIME + NEXT + WEEK + I + FINISH + SEE + MOVIE
(82b) signs of ALL + FINISH + NOW (THIS) + TIME + NEXT + WEEK + SEE + MOVIE

Literally translated, (82a) means "By this time next week I will have seen the movie." *Gone* is of course not used nor even implied in this version but the restructuring of the sentence eliminates the need for it. *Finish* expresses *will have*, while *see* in this particular configuration implies *seen*. The whole expression depends on the initial phrase, *now + time + next + week*, which expresses that the action will be completed by a certain time next week. (82b) is not quite as clear as version (82a) since it implies a slightly different sense by not using a personal pronoun and by placing the sign for *finish* after *all.* It translates something like: "Everything will be finished by this time next week and I will see the movie."

Modal auxiliaries, although without any formal signs, are expressed by the use of substitute signs or circumlocutions. Oddly enough, a few of these modals are not difficult in the least for the monks, perhaps because they interpret the meanings of them before actually signing their silent equivalents. For example, *may* expresses permission in speech; the monks simple sign it as *please + give + me + indulgence,* or "please grant me permission." *Would* and *can* are expressed in the signs as *wood; could* is designated by the same signs for *may* since both imply permission. *Might* cannot be expressed:

(83) I think I might go to the refectory tonight.
(83a) signs of I + THINK + I + GO + TWO + EAT + HOUSE + THIS + NIGHT

(84) May I go to the refectory?
(84a) signs of PLEASE + GIVE + ME + INDULGENCE + TWO + GO + TWO + EAT + HOUSE + QUESTION MARK

(85) Can I go to work?
(85a) signs of WOOD + YOU + GIVE + ME + INDULGENCE + TWO + GO + TWO + WORK

(85b) signs of WOOD + YOU + LIKE + TWO + GIVE + ME + INDULGENCE + TWO + GO + TWO + WORK

(86) Would you like to read in the library?
(86a) signs of WOOD + YOU + WANT + TWO + READ + UNDER + BOOK + HOUSE

(87) I would be happy to.
(87a) signs of I + WOOD + B + HAPPY + TWO

(88) Could you (abbot) give me permission to go to Rome?
(88a) signs of ABBOT + YOU + THINK + UP + TWO + YOU + TWO + GIVE + ME + INDULGENCE + TWO + GO + TWO + POPE + COURTYARD

(89) I ought to go.
(89a) signs of RULE + SAY + TIME + TWO + GO

(90) I had better go.
(90a) signs of I + BUTTER + GO + NOW

(91) I must go now.
(91a) signs of GOOD + FOUR + ME + TWO + GO + NOW

Without the sign for *wood* and its sound repeated in the viewer's mind, the modal auxiliary *would* would not be possible in the sign language. As noted in an earlier section, this is a fairly common occurence and quite necessary sometimes, otherwise an expression could not be signed. (90a) illustrates a similar device in *butter* for *better*. *Ought* and *should* are expressed by the same signs, although the latter modal is not illustrated here. Both imply an obligation. The signs for *rule + say* are also used to express obligation.

CONCLUSION

This brief review of some of the major characteristics of the Cistercian sign language leads one to many observations and conclusions, particularly in regard to its effectiveness as a means of silent communication. Although this sign language, as others, is lacking in many of the grammatical elements necessary for expressing the nuances of thought, it does function very effectively within the context of the monastic life. Simple statements and questions are possible with some leeway for more complex messages. However, one must always keep in mind that the sign language has traditionally been intended only for brief communication and to restrict communication on a wider level.

The layman, as well as the monk, has found it necessary to invent expressions to fill the gaps in language, whether that language be spoken or silent. Thus, signs have been invented spontaneously so that messages can be better expressed. Significantly, for the Cistercians the inventory of authorized signs is less than the inventory of original ones. One drawback of this is that such expressions are operative on a limited "idiolect" level and often are not understood by all monks. They add a burden to an already overburdened language.

To add to the problem is the fact that many of the brothers, particularly the older ones, do not learn new signs easily. During the course of numerous formal and informal interviews at the monastery, many of the brothers admitted quite candidly that they could not use the signs with any imagination simply because they did not wish to or because they did not have the facility to do so. This is somewhat analogous to an older person's attempt to learn a foreign language; one must study and practice it carefully and diligently to cultivate a facility in that language. So too with the sign language.

The sign language can never be an effective means of communicating complex messages, due to its many defects. However, as pointed out earlier, the sign language is intended to express only brief, silent messages.

The following list sets forth most of its deficiencies: (1) the language operates on an "idiolect-dialect" level; (2) the authorized sign inventory is quite small, restricting communication; (3) there are no definite and indefinite articles, although the sign for *one* is frequently used to express the indefinite article; (4) connectives, with the exception of *but* can be signed only with great imagination; (5) verb forms, with few exceptions, are lacking; (6) tenses are quite difficult to express, particularly past and future; (7) pronouns of all classes must be invented within the context of the message being signed; (8) adjective and adverb forms are limited and contrived; (9) number is somewhat difficult to designate since there are no plural verb and noun forms; (10) the possessive can be signed only with ingenuity; (11) nouns and verbs are used interchangeably, creating some confusion; (12) compound signs cause some garbling; (13) interrogatives must be created within the context of the conversation, one has difficulty indicating a question pattern; (14) the signs often utilize some phonological features of speech and the viewer of the message must be prepared for them; (15) negative statements and questions offer some difficulty but generally follow speech patterns; (16) long messages are quite difficult to express, particularly if they are on a high level of abstraction; (17) there is a lack of signs for objects and persons outside the monastic life, such as kinship terms for family members.

Although these are some of the defects of the sign language, one must observe that there are a number of positive features, such as its simplicity and its metaphorical nature, both of which are revealed in the two examples of "The Lord's Prayer" which follow and which aptly end this discussion.

THE LORD'S PRAYER

PRAYER + ABOUT + GOD + FATHER

Our Father, who art in Heaven, hallowed be thy name;
YOU + ME + FATHER + STAY + GOD + COURTYARD + BLESSED + B + YOU + NAME
   thy kingdom come, thy will be done,
YOU + KING + COURTYARD + COME + YOU + W + B + ARRANGE
   on earth as it is in Heaven. Give us
THIS + DIRT + COURTYARD + SAME + GOD + COURTYARD. GIVE + YOU + ME
   this day our daily bread, and forgive us
THIS + DAY + YOU + ME + DAY + BREAD + FOUR + GIVE + YOU + ME
   our trespasses as we forgive those who trespass against us.
SIN + SAME + YOU + ME + FOUR + GIVE + SIN + ARRANGE + FAULT.
   And lead us not into temptation but deliver us from evil
NO + ARRANGE + SIN + ALL + SAME + UNLOAD + YOU + ME + HARD + TIME
   For thine is the kingdom and the power and the glory forever.
FOUR + YOU + COURTYARD + POWER + LIGHT + FOUR + ALL + TIME

Amen

FINISH

Our Father, who art in Heaven, hallowed be thy name;
GOD + ABBOT + CHARGE + BLESS + CLOISTER + BLESS + YOU + NAME
   thy kingdom come, thy will be done,
YOU + PEACE + COME + YOU + RULE + WORK
   on earth as it is in Heaven.
HERE + SAME + BLESS + CLOISTER.
   Give us this day our daily bread, and forgive us our trespasses
GIVE + ALL + BREAD + TODAY + FOUR + GIVE + ALL + FAULTS
   as we forgive those who trespass against us.
SAME + BROTHER + FOUR + GIVE + BROTHER + FAULT.
   And lead us not into temptation but deliver us from evil
HELP + ALL + WAIT + SEPARATE + BAD + RULE + HELP + ALL + WORK +
      GOOD + RULE
   For thine is the kingdom and the power and the glory forever.
YOU + CHARGE + ALL + YOU + ALL + STRONG + YOU + GIVE + ALL + LIGHT +
      ALL + TIME

Amen

FINISH

A Dictionary of the
Cistercian Sign Language

INTRODUCTION

DICTIONARIES serve many purposes, but most significantly they are exact records of the historical evolution of languages, the etymologies and meanings of the words that are essential components of man's greatest achievement: language. Although this "Dictionary of the Cistercian Sign Language" is in no way as diverse and profound as most dictionaries, it is similar in at least two ways: (1) it is an historical record of a language and its components: signs; and (2) it is a guide to usage, albeit somewhat sketchy. Unfortunately, there is little or no information on the evolution of the signs as a group or individually. Indeed, the origin of the signs is lost in antiquity; to try to trace their development and influence is a nearly impossible task. Happily, a few sign lists are still extant and some enterprising scholar could conceivably compile an authoritative list from the manuscripts in the various monasteries and libraries throughout Europe and Great Britain. Any work of this sort would be an enormous contribution to scholarship. This dictionary is only a beginning because it does record for posterity the meanings and physical configurations of the signs as they are traditionally used within the Cistercian Order.

As a guide to the use of the signs, this dictionary serves only to identify the signs, their meaning or meanings, and their physical configurations. Since so many of the signs can be used interchangeably as nouns or verbs, only a very few are actually marked as those parts of speech, usually to differentiate similar signs, such as *ring* (a) and *ring* (to). Just how the monks put these signs together into a meaningful pattern will depend on the individual monks and their facility with the silent language, an observation that has been made several times in the earlier parts of this volume. One should also note that, as a guide to usage, this dictionary quite specifically states in what manner individual signs are put together into more complex signs, according to traditional usages within the Order. This is very specific in the "Authorized List of Signs for the Cistercian"; the monks must use the signs in exactly the manner stated. To the more conservative of the brothers, this requirement of making the signs exactly as given in the Order's official list would be followed to the letter. In fact, the translation of the official list from French, as noted above, was made precisely as the signs are signaled in France, preserving the French word-order. The English translation of the official list, as presented in this dictionary, attempts to reproduce the list exactly as it occurs in the *Usages* of 1926, for the benefit of those who wish to still maintain traditional signs and the ways they are made.

If this dictionary is a guide to the traditional signs of the Cistercian Order, it is also an illustration of the limitations of the sign language. If it is not constantly up-dated to include new signs for new items introduced into the monastery, it will slowly degenerate until speech results. And this is, indeed, what has happened; speech is obviously taking precedence.

To support this thesis, the dictionary has been divided into three major sections, as follows: (a) "Authorized List of Signs for the Cistercian Order"; (b) "Authorized List of Signs for St Joseph's Abbey"; and a (c) "List of Original Signs from St Joseph's Abbey." Each section, except the original signs, is further subdivided into "common" and "uncommon" signs, the latter marked with an asterisk (*). (a) represents the greater language level, the standard if you wish; (b) signifies the dialect level; and (c) denotes the idiolect level. A fourth level is implied by the increasing use of speech within the monasteries, a natural result of the ever present need of men to communicate effectively and immediately.

The reason for this breakdown of the sign language is quite obvious: change, or lack of it. Since the official list has never been up-dated by the Order to include newer, more relevant signs, the brothers find it necessary to modify the official signs or invent new ones which, in the case of St Joseph's Abbey, are authorized by that Abbey for use only in that monastery. One notes very quickly that some of the official signs of the Order are presented in the Abbey's list but in slightly different forms: dialect forms. Such signs oftentimes vary in the order of the elements of the signs, or are simpler forms of official signs with more than one element. Even the physical configurations of the Abbey's versions of the official signs vary somewhat. Moreover, the way of making official signs also varies from house to house, a fact which often hinders silent communication among monks from different monasteries.

However, even the signs authorized by the Abbey are not always sufficient to facilitate communication; so the monks take it one step further and invent signs on the spur of the moment to communicate some message that would otherwise be uncommunicable. Thus, we have the "original" or "useless" signs that are illustrative of the idiolect level of the sign language. It is these signs which are most relevant to the brothers even though they are not part of the permanent vocabulary of either the official list or the Abbey's list. Such signs are constantly being invented for immediate purposes and rarely gain recognition beyond the exchange in which they are used.

The final stage in the breakdown of the sign language from the idiolect level is toward speech. Perhaps it is an inevitable step given the ever increasing emphasis on verbal dialogue among the brothers. If the religious are to develop their personalities and expand their mutual understanding of each other, then speech, in limited conversation, is necessary. It would be unfortunate, however, if the signs were eliminated altogether, for it is through them that some silence can be maintained. In a life dedicated to true prayer and recollection, too much emphasis on speech could prove to be a danger to that life and the concepts behind it for "In silence did I find Thee."

ORGANIZATION OF THE DICTIONARY

As stated above, the organization of this dictionary reflects the various levels of the sign language as well as the stages through which the language passes before it breaks down completely. However this might be, the dictionary has a very practical use for those houses that still observe and teach the signs: it can be used as a source for meanings and configurations. By using the dictionary, the religious can better standardize the signs and their usage. Although such a work cannot prevent the formation of dialect and ideolect forms, it will at least offer some norm by which the monks might better utilize the signs.

There are three sections to this dictionary, the first of which takes precedence over the others. The "Authorized List of Signs for the Cistercian Order" is the list that must be followed if a particular monastery does not have a list of its own to follow. It is the traditional list and reflects the traditional way of life in the Cistercian monastery. However, the signs are not all up-to-date, in the sense that many of them reflect the things of the past centuries that are not longer used in the monastery. These are marked as "Uncommon" signs by an asterisk; that is, they no longer have relevance to the religious within the monastery simply because newer, more modern items have been added. Nonetheless, they are reproduced because they are parts of the list that cannot be removed. This then is the first section of the dictionary.

The second major section contains the "Authorized List of Signs for St Joseph's Abbey." Most of these signs are duplicates of the official list, some exact, and some dialect forms which have been approved by the abbey for use *only* in that monastery. One should also note that there are many signs which are peculiar to that abbey and reflect that abbey's equipment and physical plant, as well as some of the products they manufacture.

The last, and largest section, is the "List of Original Signs" that mirrors the daily activities and preoccupations of the brothers of St Joseph's Abbey. In many ways, these signs are ingenious inventions that help fill the gaps in the traditional list's meager inventory. However, such signs must be used with discretion for within the context of the monastic life and ideal they can be corrosive; thus, the term "useless" which is used interchangeably with "original." This list is not divided into "Common" and "Uncommon" signs, for they are neither; each is unique. They indicate the need to communicate more complete messages and touches of humor. These signs are personal ones invented on the spur of the moment and are not valid for other monasteries. The brothers of St Joseph's Abbey are able to understand them because they have developed a rapport among themselves; they can recognize each other's "style," so to speak.

In addition to these three major divisions, the dictionary is further divided into "Basic" or "Simple" signs, and "Derived" or "Compound" signs. Each section, except the "Original" sign list, is sub-divided into these types of signs for ease of photographing. Also, since "Derived" signs are made up of "Basic" signs, one can learn them easily by first learning the elements that comprise them. We have selected the term "Derived" because such signs are literally derived from the "Basic" signs which contain only one element but which are the building blocks of the more complex signs.

The Manner of Making the Signs

Used in the Cistercian Order[1]

In making the signs, the right hand is always used when only one hand is necessary; and when one finger is sufficient, the forefinger is always used, unless another is specially mentioned. Noises with the mouth, in order to make the signs understood, are absolutely forbidden. The days of the week are counted by *one* finger for Sunday, *two* for Monday, and so on. To signify a room, workshop, etc.,the sign of *house* is made, and that of the person.

---

[1] Quoted from *Regulations of the Order of Cistercians of the Strict Observance* (Dublin, 1926), p. 137.

Authorized List of Signs for the Cistercian Order

BASIC SIGNS

A

abbot

touch the upper right forehead vertically with tips of right forefinger and middle finger held tightly together

acid

with the tip of the right forefinger scratch Adam's Apple (throat); back of hand forward and chin slightly downwards

acolyte

make the sign of CHOIR RELIGIOUS or NOVICE, and place right palm under left elbow (left forearm vertical) then raise and lower left forearm with right palm still in contact; back of left hand forward and left forefinger extended

after

place right hand near right hip with palm facing backwards; draw hand back and forth several times

alb

pinch the cowl or robe near the right knee with right forefinger and thumb

all

move right fist several times from left to right quickly at just below chest level; back of hand is up

amice

make the sign of LINEN, and then place open right hand, palm down, on top of head; fingers point left

animal

place middle joint of right forefinger sidewards on tip of nose and move curved finger up and down

apple

turn tip of right little finger into open palm of left hand

apron
place fingertips of both hands at sides then draw them around as though putting on an apron

*ass
sign of ANIMAL, then put tip of right thumb on right ear with palm forward and move fingers up and down

assistant
place fingertips of both hands at sides then draw them around as though putting on an apron

B

bad
hold tip of nose with thumb and forefinger of right hand, then drop them quickly

balance
extend both hands out before body with palms up, then raise and lower them alternately

basket
with right forefinger describe a circle horizontally in front of body, then raise both fists as though lifting the two handles of a basket

beads
pass the right forefinger and thumb over tip of the left forefinger several times

beautiful
pass palm of right hand downward in front of face; right elbow is at right angle to side of body

before
place right hand near right hip with palm forward, then bring hand forward; fingers are pointed down

*bellows
join hands palm to palm then open and close them like a bellows with heels of hands always in contact

belt
hold hands (fists) at sides then bring them around to stomach

big
hold hands near sides of head with palms pointed toward head and with fingers spread apart

bind (to)
join the thumb and forefinger of each hand and turn them around one another; then separate the hands slowly as though tying a knot

bishop
trace a cross on chest with right fore-finger; for the Bishop of the Diocese, add sign of HERE

bitter
with tip of right forefinger scratch Adam's Apple (throat); back of hand forward and chin slightly downwards

black
place right forefinger sideways under nose; finger pointed stiffly to left

bless (to)
trace cross in air with right hand: (1) heel of hand downward and moved in towards body, then (2) hand moved to left then to right

blessing

same as BLESS (to)

blind
cover both eyes with the thumb and
forefingers of both hands

boil (to)
raise and lower hands alternately with
the fingers joined in a pear-shaped
configuration; back of hand forward

book
place heels of hands together then open
and close them like a book

box
place hands at side of chest (slightly
before it) with palms facing inward
toward each other, then move them so
that palms face inward toward chest
one in front of the other with space
in between; actually describing shape
of a box

bread
touch tips of forefingers and thumbs of
both hands with fingers held into palm,
then hold configuration in horizontal
position but slightly tilted forward

break (to)
place thumb side of both hands next
to each other and move them outward
and downward as though snapping
a twig

broom
move the outstretched right hand from
right to left as though sweeping with
that hand, then add the sign of WOOD
or STRAW

brush
rub right fist on left forearm several
times

butter
hold left hand out with palm up and
strike the palm gently several times
in brushing motion with tips of right
hand fingers

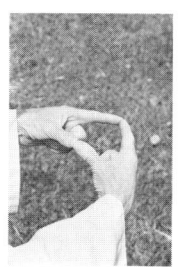

Cistercian Order: Basic Signs

*button

place tip of left forefinger on middle joint of left middle finger, then insert tip of right thumb into the opening

C

cabbage

clasp head with both hands and add sign of VEGETABLE

calotte

place tips of forefinger, middle finger and thumb of right hand on top of head but slightly set back

candlestick*

sign of LIGHT, then insert tip of right forefinger in opening formed by left fist; forefinger pointed directly downward

carpenter

move arms as though using a plane, and add sign of LAY BROTHER or SECULAR

cart

hold out hands next to each other with thumb sides up, then move hands forward and turn thumb around each other as hands move

case

same as BOX

cat

twist an imaginary moustache at sides of upper lip with tips of right and left thumb and forefinger, then add sign of ANIMAL

cellarer

extend thumb from right fist, then move tip of thumb up and down; back of hand facing right

ceremonies, master of
join tips of little fingers without separating them; other fingers are held into palms

change (to)
place open hands in front of the chest with palms facing inward, then pass one over the other alternately

chant (to)
move tip of right forefinger around open mouth but not in contact with it

chapter
join fingers of right hand in pear-shaped configuration then extend left hand with palm down, then place tips of right fingers into palm of left hand

charge
place palm of right hand on left shoulder

chasuble
raise hands from about chest level and place on respective shoulders; elbows are out to sides

cheese
place palms of hands together and twist them gently against each other a few times

child
place tip of right little finger between the lips and move several times

choir religious
with tips of right forefinger and thumb pinch scapular at chest level

church

join fingertips of both hands so that they are shaped like a roof, then hold configuration over head; or use signs of PRAY and HOUSE

cloak (of lay brothers and novices)

fully extend both arms in front of body then cross them on chest so that hands are on opposite shoulders

close (shut)

hold arms at sides then press them against sides of body

clothes

bring hands to respective shoulders as though putting on a garment; for any particular garment point to it

cold

hold both hands out in front of body with fingers bent slightly into palms, then make them tremble a little; back of hands down

come (to)

from closed right fist extend forefinger, then move forefinger back and forth a few times; back of hand forward

common

same as ALL

communion

join tips of right forefinger and thumb, then place them in contact with tongue; back of hand forward and elbow extended to side; fingers form a small circle

confusion

twirl hands around each other several times

cook
extend right fist in front of body, then move it back and forth quickly as though holding and moving a frying pan on a stove

corn
with two fists extended slightly in front of body rub fingers together rapidly; heels of hands down

cotton*
hold out left palm (up) and make believe one is raking it with the fingers of the right hand

count (to)
hold out left fingers, then touch them with right forefinger as though counting on them; or hold out left palm and make believe counting money into that palm

courtyard
join tips of forefingers, then separate them and move them back to respective sides of body forming a semi-circle as they are moved

cowl
point to it, or take hold of left sleeve under wrist with tips of right forefinger and thumb and lower right hand under left wrist

cross
hold up left forefinger with back of hand forward then place extended right forefinger over it forming a cross

crozier
hold right fist up and extend forefinger so that it is shaped like a hook; back of hand facing backward

crucifix
same as CROSS

cut (to)
extend left forefinger, then pass right forefinger over it as though cutting it

D

day
place tip of right forefinger into right cheek

deacon
draw a line from the left shoulder to the right hip with tips of right forefinger and thumb; right forefinger may be used singly as alternate way of making sign

dead
place tip of right thumb under chin raising it a bit

deaf
place palm of right hand over right ear

devil
sign of WING, then strike the forehead with tip of right forefinger several times

discipline
move right hand several times from shoulder to shoulder; hand closed as though holding a whip with tip of thumb held against the inside of forefinger

disengaged
hold out left forearm in front of body, then cross right forearm over it

dish
describe a circle over the open palm of left hand with tip of right forefinger

displeased
bring together tips of little fingers several times in front of body; backs of hands forward; other fingers pressed into palm

doctor
sign of CHOIR RELIGIOUS or SECULAR, then place tip of right forefinger on upper forearm as though bleeding it

dog
sign of ANIMAL, then pull on bottom of right earlobe with tips of right forefinger and thumb

*drawers
as though putting a pair of drawers on; body is bent over with arms extended then arms are brought up to waist level

dress (to), (wounds)
turn closed right hand around left forearm as though wrapping a bandage

drink
place tip of right thumb on lips with hand closed then tilt head backward slightly as though taking a drink

dry
strike the back of the left hand with tip of right forefinger which is vertical and extended from fist

dunghill
close right hand then rub right temple with knuckles

dust
hold out right hand with heel forward, then blow on back of it

E

eat (to)

bring thumb, forefinger and middle finger to the mouth several times; fingers are touching at tips only

edible*

pass extended right forefinger over extended left forefinger as though scraping it

egg

hold out left forefinger from fist, then scratch lower part of it with tip of right forefinger

employment

place palm of right hand on left shoulder

empty

hold left forearm vertical with hand closed and back of hand forward, then gently rub palm of right hand from left elbow to the fist (fingers of left hand may be extended)

end

place both hands together, then tap tips of forefingers several times without separating hands

equal

rub sides of forefingers together several times

evening

place tip of right forefinger over closed right eye

everything

move right fist several times from left to right quickly at just below chest level but slightly to side of body

extinguish (to)
cover left forefinger with thumb and first two fingers of right hand

extinguisher
same as EXTINGUISH (to)

F

fast (to)
press lips together with sides of right thumb and forefinger

fault
strike chest with right fist several times; back of fist forward

fever
place tips right forefinger and middle finger on inner side of left wrist as though taking pulse

finish
place both hands together, then tap tips of forefingers several times without separating hands

fire
hold up tip of forefinger then blow on it

fish
move right hand forward in a zig-zag motion; palm facing left and fingers held together

flour
turn right forefinger and middle finger down from fist, then rub right thumb against them, and add sign of CORN

flower

hold tips of right thumb, forefinger and middle finger together, then bring them to nose as though smelling them

fruit

strike left elbow with palm of right hand; left forearm is vertical with fist closed

G

gather (to)

hold out right hand with forefinger and middle finger down, then move thumb against them several times and moving the hand as though picking something; other fingers are held into palm

girdle*

bring the closed hands from sides of body to stomach

give (to)

push forward open right hand with palm up and fingers held together tightly

glass

scratch front teeth with tip of right forefinger

glue

sign of THICK, then pass fingers (right) over the left hand as if using a brush

go (to)

make a sweep outward from body with right hand; fingers come up as this is performed

God

form a verticle triangle with tips of thumbs and forefingers; other fingers pressed into palms

good
place right hand on chest with palm open, then move it up and down several times while still in contact with chest

grain
place nail of right little finger on right thumbnail; move little finger on the thumbnail slightly

grass
hold out both hands with palms facing, fingers stiff, then move them up and down alternately as though chopping something

green
with tip of right forefinger draw a line from ear to nose

gun
raise two hands to the shoulder as though holding a rifle

H

habit
bring hands to respective shoulders as though putting on a garment; for any particular garment point to it

half
hold out left forefinger from fist, then touch middle knuckle with tip of right forefinger

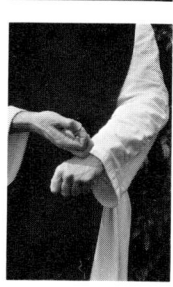

*handkerchief
sign of BAD, then pass open right hand downward over chest as though wiping fingers on chest

hard
strike back of left hand with middle knuckle of right middle finger

hear (to)
strike the right ear with tip of little finger of right hand several times

heart
with tips of both forefingers draw a heart over the heart

heat
hold out right hand with palm open, then blow on it lightly

help
place fingertips on stomach, then draw them back in opposite directions to sides

*herb
hold out both hands with heels down, fingers stiff, then move hands up and down alternately as though chopping something

here
point extended right forefinger towards the ground several times

hide
put the open right hand under the left armpit several times

hood*
sign of CLOTHES, then place the edge of right hand on the chest

horse
sign of ANIMAL, then pull hair directly above middle of forehead with right hand but with fingers slightly closed

hot
hold out right hand with palm open,
then blow on it lightly

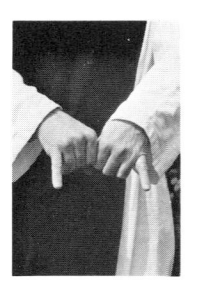

hour
place thumb sides of both fists together
then extend little fingers without
fists separating

house
join tips of fingers of both hands in
shape of a roof

hundred
place tip of extended right forefinger
into open mouth but not in contact
with it

I

I (myself)
touch tip of right forefinger on chest

idle
hold out left forearm in front of body,
then cross right forearm over it

incense (to)
hold out closed right hand with fingers
pointing downward, then move hand
as though incensing

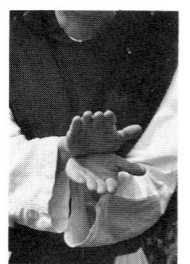

incense-boat
hold out open left hand then place
open right hand over it; then move
right hand from heel like a hinge
several times

indulgence
trace a circle on the stomach with tip
of right forefinger

invitator

place tip of right thumb between the right forefinger and middle finger; hold tightly

iron

pass the first two fingers of right hand over the left forefinger several times as though filing a piece of metal, then add sign of HARD

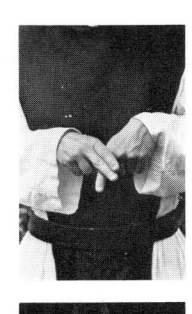

J

*jug

raise right hand, closing it as though grasping a jug or handle, then make sign of WATER

K

key

hold out right hand as though holding a key, then turn hand as though turning a key in a lock

knife

pass right forefinger over left wrist then add sign of CUT

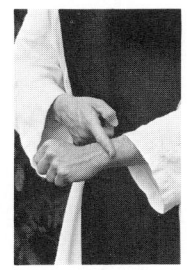

L

ladder

raise the two hands one after the other as though climbing a ladder

late

with the tip of the right forefinger scratch between the eyes

lavabo towel

make the sign of LINEN, then move the right forefinger and thumb as the priest does at the lavabo

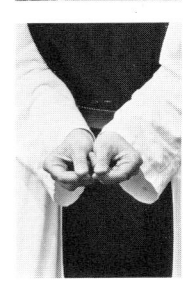

lay brother

take hold of the beard, or an imaginary one, with right closed hand then pull on beard slightly

leather

pinch the skin of the back of the left hand with tips of right forefinger and thumb

leek

sign of VEGETABLE, then place right forefinger and middle finger on left forearm; other fingers held down by thumb

light

sign of FIRE, then raise right forefinger above face

*linen

extend hands horizontally, palms down, then add the sign of THREAD

little

tap tip of right forefinger on tip of right thumb

load

place right hand, palm open, on left shoulder

long

hold out left fist, then place right forefinger and thumb on it, then move right away from it as though pulling a piece of thread from left hand

low

hold out open right hand, palm down, near to the ground

M

maniple*

place right hand under left forearm

manure
rub right temple with knuckles of
right fist

mass
place thumbs on forefingers, then hold
heels of hands together and raise hands
together slowly as though raising host

master of novices
place tip of right thumb on tip of
left little finger

match
place tip of right forefinger at the
bottom of left forefinger, then make
sign of FIRE

meat
pinch skin of left hand just below
thumb with side of right forefinger
and thumb

medicine*
pass open right hand over the chest
several times from right to left; tips of
fingers pointing left

metal
hold out left forefinger, then pass
forefinger and middle finger of right
hand down over it several times as
though filing a piece of metal, then
add sign of HARD

milk
hold out left forefinger so that tip is
pointing down, then grasp it with right
hand as though milking a cow

*mill
move thumbs around one another
several times, then add sign of HOUSE

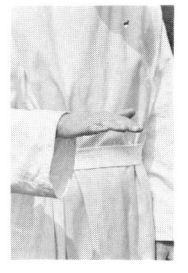

mistaken (to be)
hold out right hand with palm up, then turn hand over so that palm is facing down

month
strike the inside of bent left elbow with edge of right hand

morning
place tip of right forefinger on lower eyelid of right eye

*mow
stretch arms before body as though holding a scythe, then move arms as though actually cutting with the scythe

much
with tip of right forefinger draw a line from left shoulder to right shoulder across chest

much (too much)
with edge of right hand draw a line across the throat

N

needle
with tip of right forefinger point to the middle joint of left forefinger, then add sign of SEW

night
place tip of right forefinger over closed left eye and tip of thumb over closed right eye

none
make sign of OFFICE, then point to the bottom of the left forefinger with tip of right forefinger

nothing
shake right hand loosely at side of body

novice
extend right forefinger and middle finger and place them near right ear, preferably behind it; thumb and other fingers are pressed into palm, then add sign of CHOIR RELIGIOUS or LAY BROTHER

nut
hold out left thumb in vertical position with inside tip facing forward, then grasp it from behind with tips of right forefinger and thumb; right thumb on left side of left thumb, then add sign of HARD

oblate   O

sign of NOVICE or LAY BROTHER, then strike right side of right knee with edge of right hand, palm up

oil
pass extended right forefinger across closed lips; tip of forefinger pointing left

onion
sign of VEGETABLE, then rub right eye with thumb side of closed right hand

ordo
sign of BOOK, then place palm of right hand on the back of extended left hand, palm down

ox*
sign of ANIMAL, then extend both forefingers from fists and place on sides of head, near forehead (temples) like horns

P

paper
hold out open left hand with palm down, then rub back of right hand over it several times

paste
sign of THICK, then pass right fingers over left palm as though brushing something

pax, instrument of the
bring right fist to mouth and kiss knuckles of forefinger and middle finger; back of hand forward

pear
turn tip of right thumb into open palm of left hand

*penknife
hold out left forefinger, then make believe you are sharpening it with tips of right forefinger and thumb

pick (to)
hold out right hand with forefinger and middle finger down, then move them several times up and down and simultaneously moving hand with picking motion; other fingers held into palm

pig
sign of ANIMAL, then turn tip of right forefinger into right side of nose

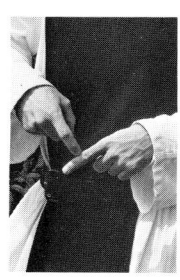

pin
push tip of right forefinger into side of left forefinger several times

plate
sign of DISH, then place tip of right forefinger into middle of left palm

pluck
join closed fists at knee level then pull them up quickly as though pulling at something

plum
grasp bottom of left forefinger with right thumb and forefinger then add sign of SOFT

poor
hold out right hand with palm up as though begging; fingers are curved in slightly

pope
draw three circles over the head with tip of right forefinger; as each is made the next is made slightly smaller

pot*
sign of DISH, then place right palm on left palm which is facing up

potato
turn tip of right forefinger on palm of left hand

pray
interlace fingers of both hands

prayer, mental prayer
same as PRAY

president
with palm of right hand forward raise middle finger with other fingers held down by thumb

*prime
sign of OFFICE, then extend left forefinger and place tip of right forefinger on left forefinger's nail

prior
close right hand and raise thumb
stiffly from fist

professed
link both forefingers together

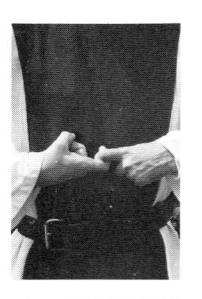

prostration*
cross the arms on the chest, then incline
the trunk slightly, as if to prostrate

psalm
place tip of right thumb on lips, then
wriggle the fingers at the same time

pull up
place fists at knee, then quickly pull them up
as though pulling up something

purple
place right forefinger and middle finger
on forehead with tips facing left

Q

quarter
pass the tip of the right forefinger over
the first joint of the left forefinger

quick
strike the two fists sharply together

quickly
same as QUICK

R

rain

join fingers of each hand in pear shaped configuration, then raise and lower them alternately; fingers pointed down

rake

curve fingers of right hand with palm down, then draw hand towards oneself

*rank

move the hands forward parallel with one another, then place end (edge) of the right hand on the palm of the left

razor

sign of KNIFE, then curve right forefinger and pass side of it down over the right cheek as though shaving

red

place tip of right forefinger on lower lip and bend lip slightly

relics

with tips of right forefinger and middle finger pinch skin on back of left hand, then raise both and kiss them

religious

with tips of right forefinger and thumb pinch scapular at chest level

remain (to)

stretch out open right hand with palm down, then move it downwards

*remedy

pass open right hand over chest several times from right to left; tips of fingers pointing left

reprimand

scratch the cheek near the right ear
with all fingers of right hand; motion
is downwards

ring (a)

show the first joint of the ring finger
(third finger, left hand)

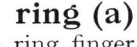

ring (to)

move the right arm up and down as
though pulling on a bell rope

ripe

push the tip of right thumb into
fleshy part of left hand several times

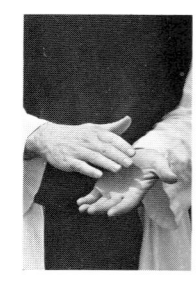

ripen (to)

same as RIPE

*rising, signal for rising

strike the open left palm several times
with the tips of the fingers of the right
hand

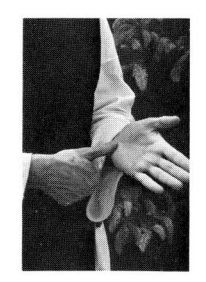

roots

pass the right forefinger over the
extended left forefinger several times
as though scraping it

rosary

pass the tip of the right thumb over
the first joint of the right forefinger
several times as though counting beads

rule

pass the palm of the right hand over
the left little finger

S

sacraments, last

hold out left hand with palm up then draw a cross on it with tip of right thumb

saint

sign of PRAY, then look up to heaven

salt

rub tip of tongue with tip of right forefinger

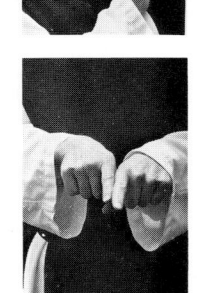

salt-cellar*

trace a small circle on left hand with tip of right forefinger, then add sign of SALT

same as

rub sides of forefingers together; other fingers held into palms

sand

turn right forefinger and middle finger down, then rub tip of right thumb against them, then point down to the ground

saw

pass edge of right hand over wrist of left hand as though sawing something

scales

hold out hands side by side with palms up, then move them up and down alternately

scissors

right forefinger and middle finger move forward as though cutting something with a pair of scissors; fingers move against each other as the hand moves forward

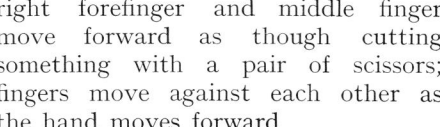

scold (to)
scratch right cheek near right ear with fingers of right hand; motion is downwards

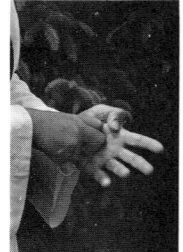

seal
bend right forefinger and middle finger, then press middle joints into palm of left hand

secular
pass nail or side of right thumb down over mouth and chin; rest of hand is closed

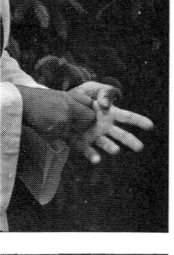

see (to)
put tip of right forefinger beneath right eye, then move finger forward

seed
place nail of right little finger on right thumbnail and move them against each other slightly

serpent
move the right forefinger forward in a zig-zag motion

serve (to)
pass the hands around body as though putting on an apron; motion is from front of body to back or sides

service
kiss the back of the right hand

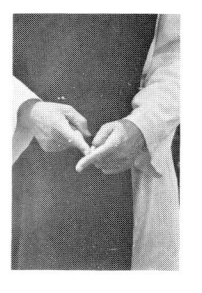

sext
sign of OFFICE, then point to middle joint of left forefinger with tip of right forefinger

shame

place palm of right hand over both eyes

shoe

show the right foot, then pinch the skin on the back of the right hand

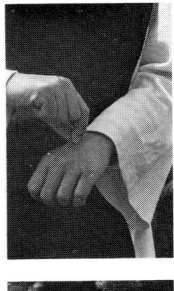

*shoemaker

bring the closed hands together, turn them downwards and separate them sharply

shovel

extend the open right hand in front of body, then lower it

sick

lean to one side, keeping right elbow close to right side and the hand raised and closed

sickle*

hold up left fist, then move right hand under it as though cutting with a sickle

*silk

hold right forefinger and thumb to mouth, then withdraw them slowly

sing (to)

move tip of right forefinger around, but not in contact with, open mouth

sleep (to)

place palm of right hand on right side of face then lean to right side on that hand with hand still in contact with head

snake
move the right forefinger forward in a
zig-zag motion

*snuff
sign of FLOUR, then bring right
fingers to the nose as though taking
snuff

soap
rub right cheek with right fist, then add
sign of HARD

socks
place tip of right forefinger between
the foot and the shoe

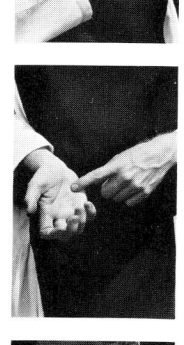

soft
with tip of right forefinger feel the
fleshy part of left hand, just below the
little finger

soldier
bring right fist to left hip, then draw
it across body as though drawing a
sword

soon
move the tip of the right forefinger on
the end of the thumb of the same hand

soul
place right hand on forehead, then
raise it, looking upwards

soup
hold out left fist with thumb side up,
then cover it with palm of right hand

sour

scratch the throat from the chin downwards with tip of right forefinger

spade

move the arms as though digging with a shovel and move feet with the appropriate motions

speak (to)

place the tip of right forefinger to the mouth

spectacles

form circles with the thumbs and forefingers of both hands, then place them over the eyes

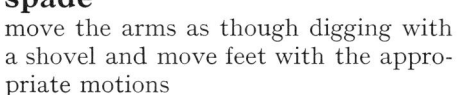

spoon

bring right forefinger and middle finger to mouth as though using a spoon

spread (to)

stretch the hands out flat, then separate them, keeping them on same plane

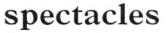

stand (to)

hold out right hand with palm up, then raise it sharply several times

stand up (to)

same as STAND

*stockings

sign of WOOL, then make believe putting them on

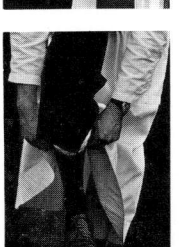

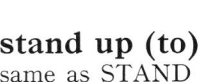

stole
bring the two forefingers from the neck
to the chest then cross them on chest

stone
bend right forefinger and middle finger,
then strike the right side of the head
several times

strong
raise right arm at side of body with
fist as though showing how strong
you are

sub-prior
extend thumb and little finger from
right fist

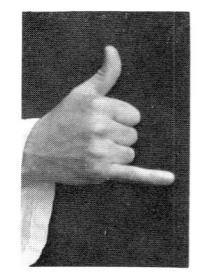

sweet
put tip of right forefinger between
pursed lips and move them gently

T

table
hold out both hands with palms down,
then separate them so that each hand
moves to respective side, then add
sign of WOOD, if table is wooden

take (to)
hold out right hand with palm down,
then move it in toward body and close
hand slightly as this is done

tall
put the right hand out with palm down
then raise it to indicate height

tear (to)
place thumb sides of both hands next
to each other, then move them outward
and down as though snapping a twig;
hands are closed at all times

thank (to)
bring hand to mouth as though about to kiss it; or kiss tips of right fingers

thanks
same as THANK

thanksgiving
place right palm over heart then raise eyes to heaven

thick
hold out right hand with fingers joined at tips and pointing up, then separate them several times hitting the thumb

thin
spread fingers of both hands with palms facing downwards, then place fingers of right hand into spread fingers of left

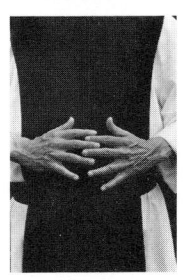

thread
draw a straight line from tip of left forefinger with tips of right forefinger and thumb, then describe several circles around left thumb and forefinger

thurible
raise the hand as though incensing

tie (to)
same as BIND

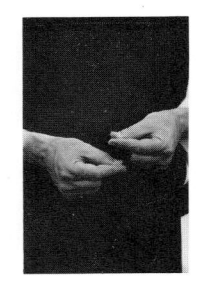

tierce
sign of OFFICE, then point to first joint of left forefinger with tip of right forefinger

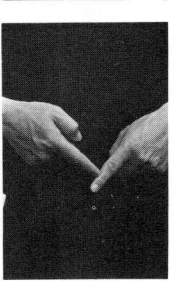

tired
drop extended forearms to sides

tomorrow
hold right fist before right shoulder, then push it forward once but slightly down as motion is made. DAY AFTER TOMORROW: make motion twice

tool
place palm of right hand on or near right shoulder, then move it forward and outwards

U

ugly
pass open right hand up from chin to forehead before face but not in contact with it

understand (to)
touch right temple with the right forefinger several times

unload (to)
place back of right hand on left shoulder, then move it forward several times with quick motion

unloaded (to be)
same as UNLOAD

useless
hold out left forearm in front of body, then cross right forearm over it

V

vegetable
hold fingers of left hand up and joined at tips, then grasp them with the right hand and draw right hand up on them, and add sign of ROOT

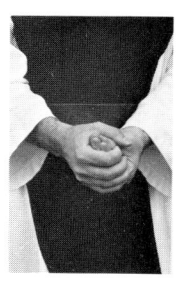

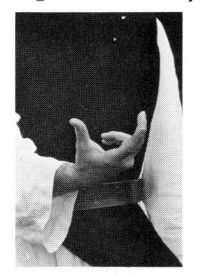

vessel

hold out forefinger, middle finger and thumb of right hand with other fingers pressed into palm and palm up; extended fingers and thumb are spread wide

W

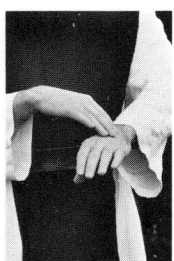

wash (to)

strike back of left hand with tips of fingers of right hand several times

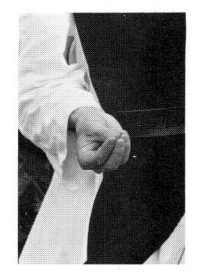

water

join tips of fingers of right hand with palm up

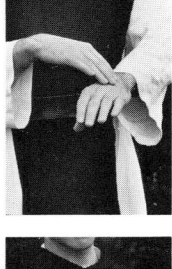

water (to)

sign of WATER, then turn fingers upside down

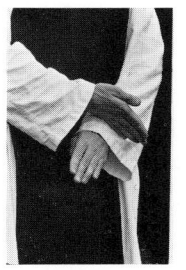

week

strike left wrist with edge of right hand

well

same as GOOD

white

place right forefinger and middle finger on mouth then move down over mouth to chin; tips of fingers are pointed up

wine

place tip of right forefinger on tip of nose from directly in front of face

wing

place tip of right thumb at right corner of mouth with fingers spread, then move fingers and hand slightly

woman
place right forefinger and middle finger on forehead with tips of fingers pointing left, then draw fingers across forehead from left to right

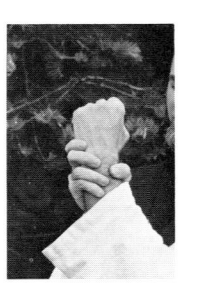

wood
hold left forearm vertical with hand closed, then grasp left wrist with right hand and move right hand around wrist while still in contact

wool
grasp material on left forearm with tips of right forearm and thumb, then pull on material

work
strike thumb side of left fist with little finger side of right fist several times

write (to)
join right forefinger, middle finger and thumb then move them from side to side as though writing with a pen or pencil

Y

*yard (of monastery)
cross one hand over the other with palms down

year
strike left shoulder with edge of right hand

yellow
place tips of right forefinger and middle finger between eyes, then draw them down over face to tip of nose; finger tips pointing up

young
same as CHILD

Authorized List of Signs for the Cistercian Order

DERIVED SIGNS

agony*
signs of DEAD and LITTLE

altar
signs of TABLE and MASS

altar-cloth
signs of LINEN and ALTAR

angel
signs of WING and SAINT

angelus
make three times sign of RINGING, then add sign of OUR LADY

antiphonal*
signs of BOOK, CHANT and MATINS

apostle
signs of SAINT, SERMON and RED

ask to (to)
make sign of THANKS and sign of object wanted, or point to it

assistant cantor
signs of SERVE and CANTOR

awaken (to)*
signs of SLEEP, then rub the eyes or make sign of FINISH

B

bag
describe a circle horizontally with tip of right forefinger, then add sign of HIDE

baker
move the closed hands up and down as though kneading dough, then make sign of LAY BROTHER or FAMILIAR

bar
take hold of left forearm with right hand, and make sign of IRON or WOOD

barn
signs of HOUSE, CART and WOOD

basin*
signs of DISH and LONG

baton*
signs of BAR and GO

beans
signs of GRAIN and EAT

bed
signs of TABLE and SLEEP

bee
signs of WING and SWEET

beef-tea*
signs of BOIL and MEAT

beer
signs of WATER and CORN

beets
signs of ROOT, RED or WHITE

bell
describe a circle horizontally with tip of right forefinger, and add sign of RING

bench
signs of TABLE and LOW

benedicite*
signs of PRAY and EAT

bier
signs of WOOD, BLACK, and DEAD

bird

signs of ANIMAL and WING

bookbinder

signs of WORK, BOOK and CHOIR RELIGIOUS or LAY BROTHER

borrow (to)

make the sign of THANKS, and that of object wanted, or point to it

bowl

signs of DISH and LONG

breviary

signs of BOOK, CHOIR RELIGIOUS and OFFICE

brick*

signs of EARTH, HARD and RED

broth*

signs of BOIL, MEAT or BUTTER

brown

signs of LAY BROTHER and PURPLE

burial

signs of SPADE and DEAD

burn

signs of FIRE and TOO MUCH

bury

signs of SPADE and DEAD

bushel

trace a circle in the air and draw a horizontal line from left to right with hand stretched out

buy (to)

signs of MONEY and GIVE

C

cabinets

signs of HOUSE and SHAME

candle (wax)*

signs of BEE and LIGHT

candle (tallow)*

signs of MEAT and LIGHT

cantor

signs of CHOIR RELIGIOUS and SING

cardboard

signs of PAPER and STRONG

carrot

signs of ROOT and YELLOW

catechism

signs of SERMON and LITTLE

cellar

signs of HOUSE and HIDE

cemetery

signs of CLOISTER, ALL and DEAD

chalice

signs of VESSEL and MASS

chapel

signs of CHURCH and SMALL

chapter, general

signs of CHAPTER, ABBOT and ALL

cherries

signs of GRAIN and RED

choir

sign of CHURCH, and that of CHOIR RELIGIOUS, LAY BROTHER or SICK, etc.

cider

signs of APPLE and WATER

clogs*

show right foot, then make sign of WOOD

cloister

describe a large semi-circle horizontally with tip of right forefinger, then add sign of CHOIR RELIGIOUS

cloth (material)

signs of LINEN, or WOOL or SILK

cloth

signs of LINEN and TABLE, or ALTAR or COMMUNION

coal*

signs of WOOD and BURN

collation

signs of EAT, LITTLE and EVENING

compline

signs of OFFICE and EVENING

conference*

signs of CLOISTER, CHOIR RELIGIOUS and SPEAK

confession

signs of FAULT and SPEAK

confessor

signs of CHOIR RELIGIOUS and CONFESSION

confessor*

signs of SAINT and WHITE

cook (to)

signs of BOIL and FINISH

cope

signs of CLOAK and BLESSING

copper

signs of METAL and RED

copse*

signs of COURTYARD, WOOD and ALL

cord

signs of THREAD and BIG

couch

signs of TABLE and SLEEP

cow

signs of OX and MILK

cress*

signs of HERB and SOUR

crozier-bearer

signs of CHOIR RELIGIOUS and CROZIER

cruet

signs of VESSEL, BLESSING, WINE and WATER

cup

signs of VESSEL and WOOD

curtain

signs of CLOTH and SLEEP

D

dessert

make sign of PORTION and show three fingers of right hand

dinner

signs of EAT and DAY

domestic*
>   signs of SERVANT and MONEY

dormitorian*
>   signs of SLEEP and CHOIR RELIGIOUS or LAY BROTHER

dormitory
>   signs of HOUSE and SLEEP

E

ember days*
>   sign of FAST and show four fingers of right hand

epistolary*
>   signs of BOOK and SUB-DEACON

F

familiar (brother)
>   signs of SERVE and SECULAR

fat*
>   signs of OIL and MEAT

feast
>   signs of DAY and IDLE

flagstones*
>   signs of EARTH, HARD and RED

forest
>   signs of COURTYARD, WOOD and ALL

freeze (to)
>   signs of WATER and HARD

frost
>   signs of WATER and HARD

G

garden
>   signs of COURTYARD and VEGETABLE

gardener
>   signs of LAY BROTHER and GARDEN

general, abbot
>   signs of ABBOT and ALL

Ghost, Holy
>   signs of GOD and WING

gospel
>   signs of BOOK and JESUS CHRIST

gospels, book of
>   signs of BOOK and DEACON

grace (after meals)
>   signs of PRAY, EAT and FINISH

gradual
>   signs of BOOK, SING and MASS

grapes
>   signs of WINE and GRAIN

grease
>   signs of OIL and MEAT

guest master
>   signs of CHOIR RELIGIOUS, SECULAR and SERVE

H

have (to)
>   show the object and make a sign of the person to whom it belongs

hay
>   signs of GRASS and DRY

hebdomadary*
    signs of PRIEST and CLOISTER

hemine*
    signs of VESSEL and CIDER, BEER or WINE

hen
    signs of BIRD and EGG

honey
    signs of BUTTER and BEE

host (sacred)
    signs of BREAD and MASS

humeral veil
    sign of CLOTHES, and hold up right fist

I

ice
    signs of WATER and HARD

incense
    signs of THURIBLE and DUST

infirmarian
    signs of CHOIR RELIGIOUS, CHARGE and SICK

injure
    signs of SICK and CUT

ink
    signs of WATER, BLACK and WRITE

instruction*
    signs of CLOISTER and SPEAK

J

Jesus Christ
    signs of GOD and CROSS

K

keeper*
king
    signs of SECULAR and GUN

    make sign of SOLDIER and describe a circle around top of head with tip of forefinger of right hand

L

Lady, Our
    signs of WOMAN and GOD

lamp
    signs of OIL and FIRE

lantern*
    signs of BOX and OIL

lauds
    signs of OFFICE and MORNING

lead
    signs of METAL and SOFT

lecture
    make the sign of BOOK, then fix eyes on outstretched hands

lent
    signs of FAST and GREAT

librarian
    signs of CHOIR RELIGIOUS, CHARGE and BOOK

lime*
    signs of STONE and BURN

M

martyr
    signs of SAINT and RED

martyrology*
signs of BOOK, SAINT and ALL

master, father (of lay brethren)
signs of MASTER OF NOVICES and LAY BROTHER

matins
signs of OFFICE and NIGHT

mattress*
signs of LINEN and STRAW

meadow
signs of COURTYARD and GRASS

meridian
signs of SLEEP and DAY

missal
signs of BOOK and MASS

O

office, divine
signs of PRAYER and SING, if sung or of SPEAK, if spoken or recited

old
signs of YEAR and MUCH, with sign of person

P

pasteboard
signs of PAPER and STRONG

peas
signs of GRAIN and EAT

pen
signs of WING and WRITE

pencil
signs of WOOD and WRITE

pepper*
signs of SALT and FLOUR

picture (holy)
signs of PAPER and SAINT. For wall pictures, add sign of BIG

plow*
signs of CART and OX

pond*
signs of WATER and FISH

porter
signs of CHOIR RELIGIOUS or LAY BROTHER, and KEY

portion*
signs of DISH and BOIL

postulant
signs of NOVICE and SECULAR

priest
signs of CHOIR RELIGIOUS or SECULAR and MASS

procession
signs of CROSS and GO

processional
signs of BOOK and PROCESSION

psalter
signs of BOOK and PSALM

R

raw
signs of FRUIT and GREEN

reader
sign of CHOIR RELIGIOUS and BOOK, then that of EAT or COMPLINE, according to whether it is for the reader in the refectory or the reader before compline

refectory
> sign of EAT and CHOIR RELIGIOUS or LAY BROTHER

regulations
> signs of BOOK and RULE

repetition
> signs of CLOISTER, CHOIR RELIGIOUS and SPEAK

rochet
> signs of LINEN, CLOTHES and SECULAR

S

sacristan*
> signs of RING (to) and CHOIR RELIGIOUS

salad
> signs of HERB and VINEGAR

scullery
> signs of HOUSE and ROOT

secretary
> signs of CHOIR RELIGIOUS and WRITE

sermon
> signs of CLOISTER and SPEAK

servant (domestic)
> signs of SERVANT and MONEY

servant, server
> signs of SERVE and CHOIR RELIGIOUS, then that of TABLE, CHURCH or MASS

shed*
> signs of HOUSE, CART and WOOD

sheep
> signs of ANIMAL and WOOL

shepherd
> signs of LAY BROTHER, CHARGE and SHEEP

shut
> signs of KEY and REMAIN; or join the hands and push them forward

shut-up (to)
> same as SHUT

silver
> signs of METAL and WHITE

smith*
> signs of LAY BROTHER or SECULAR, IRON and WORK

snuff-box*
> signs of BOX and SNUFF

spinach*
> signs of GRASS and EAT

stackyard*
> signs of HAY and COURTYARD

straw
> signs of GRASS and CORN

string
> signs of THREAD and BIG

sugar
> signs of FLOUR and SWEET

supper
> signs of EAT and EVENING

surplice*
> signs of LINEN, CLOTHES and SECULAR

sweep (to)
> signs of BROOM and WORK

T

table-cloth

signs of LINEN and of TABLE

taper*

signs of BEE and LIGHT; or MEAT and LIGHT

thrash (to)*

signs of CORN and WORK

thurifer

signs of THURIBLE, CHOIR RELIGIOUS or NOVICE

tin*

signs of METAL and WHITE

today

signs of DAY and HERE

towel

sign of LINEN, then make believe wiping hands by rubbing them together

tree

signs of WOOD and TALL

trough*

signs of WATER and OX

V

vespers

signs of OFFICE and DAY

vinegar

signs of WINE and SOUR

W

wardrobe-keeper

signs of CHOIR RELIGIOUS or LAY BROTHER, CHARGE and CLOTHES

washing

signs of WASH and HOT

wax

signs of BEE and LIGHT

woods

signs of COURTYARD, WOOD and ALL

workroom*

signs of HOUSE and ROOT

wound (to)

signs of SICK and CUT

Authorized List of Signs for St. Joseph's Abbey

BASIC SIGNS

about
extend both hands flat, palms down,
then raise and lower them alternately

acolyte
place right hand under left elbow,
raising the elbow a bit and then
extending the left forefinger

afraid
bite the fingernails of the right hand;
back of hand forward with fingers
curved in toward palm; move fingers
over teeth several times as though
biting the nails

air
blow on the back of the right hand

amice
place open right palm on top of head
with fingers pointing to the left

apple
turn tip of right little finger into open
palm of left hand

around
describe a circle horizontally with
right forefinger in front of body; tip
of finger pointed down

arrange
move fingertips of both hands down
over chest together; palms open

B

baby
place back of right hand into open
palm of left; palms are up, then move
arms from side to side gently

back
touch lower part of back with back of right hand

bar (for prying)
hold top of left wrist with palm of right hand; left knuckles down

bell
move right fist up and down as though pulling on a rope

bit
tap the tip of the right forefinger on the end of the right thumb

blue
place right forefinger and middle finger horizontally on forehead with fingers pointing left; no movement

boat
join fingertips of both hands in shape of prow and push hands forward

boots
place hands on right foot, then move hands up to about knee level as though putting on a pair of boots

brick
strike right temple with knuckles of right forefinger and middle finger

broom
place heel of right hand over thumb side of left fist, then move them in unison from side to side as though sweeping with long-handled broom

brother

place thumb side of right hand on an imaginary beard and pull down; back of hand forward

bull

place tips of right forefinger and thumb on nostrils in shape of ring with back of hand forward

buy (to)

hold out left hand, palm up, then push right thumb over right forefinger several times as though counting money into left palm

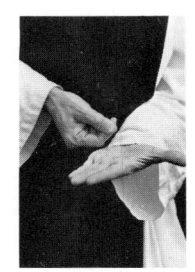

C

cat

twist an imaginary moustache at both sides of upper lip with tips of thumbs and forefingers

chain

link tips of forefingers and thumbs forming an interlocking circle, then separate them and re-make the configuration

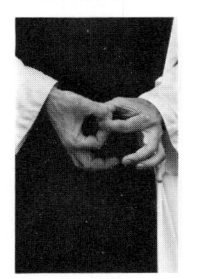

charge

place palm of right hand on left shoulder

chasuble

raise hands from about chest level and place them on respective shoulders; elbows are extended out to sides

choke

place palm of right hand on throat and squeeze a bit

chop

move open right hand diagonally from about shoulder height to about chest level (like slicing)

church

join fingertips of both hands so that they form a roof, then hold over head

cloister

describe a horizontal semi-circle with tip of right forefinger moving it from left to right or from opposite direction; finger is pointing down

close (near)

extend open hands with heels down and palms facing each other in front of body, then move them towards each other several times; no contact

coat

extend arms fully in front of body then cross them on chest so that hands are just below opposite shoulders

cook

extend right hand in front of body as though holding a pan-handle, then shake from front to back as though moving a frying pan

corner

join tips of both hands so that left hand is sideways and the right is pointing left to form a corner; back of right hand is forward and back of left is to left side

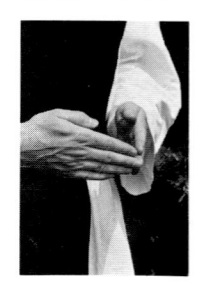

count (to)

hold out left hand with fingers spread, then touch each finger with tip of right forefinger as though counting

cow

place thumb sides of both hands on respective temples, then extend both forefingers like horns

D

dessert

strike left elbow with palm of right hand; left forearm is vertical with hand closed

devil

strike the forehead with tip of right forefinger in several places

dig (to)

churn the right hand as though digging with it; palm forward or slightly to side

dirt

rub tips of right forefinger and thumb together with other fingers extended slightly; forefinger and thumb pointed down

doctor

place tip of right forefinger on upper forearm as though giving an injection

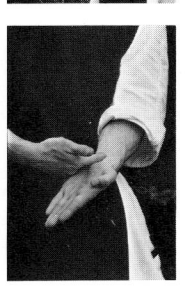

dog

pull right earlobe with tips of right forefinger and thumb

don't

shake the right hand vigorously at the right side of the body

door

hold right hand out before body with palm facing left, then move fingers back and forth like a door moving on a hinge

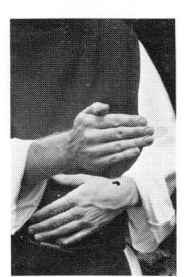

drawer (of a desk)

hold out right hand with palm up and fingers bent back almost into palm, then draw hand in toward body

drive

hold out both hands as though holding a steering wheel; then turn hands a bit as though driving an automobile

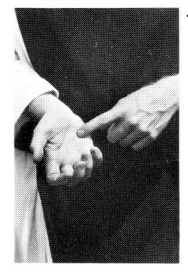

E

easy

tap soft part of left hand below thumb
with tip of right forefinger

empty

hold left forearm vertically with hand
closed and back of hand forward,
then gently pass right palm from left
elbow to fist

enough

with tip of right forefinger draw a line
across stomach from left to right

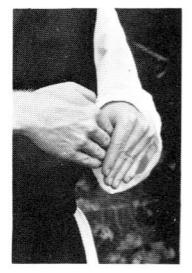

envelope

with tip of left thumb pressed against
left forefinger forming an opening,
place tips of right fingers into the
opening like placing a letter in an
envelope

exactly

hold stiff right hand at about directly
shoulder level in front of right eye, then
move hand forward and down as
though sighting a line

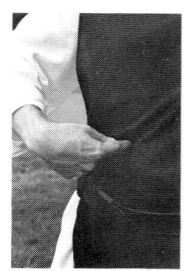

extra

with tip of right forefinger trace a
small circle on stomach

eyeglasses

form circles with tips of thumbs and
forefingers, then place them over
respective eyes

F

fast (quick)

strike closed fists together rapidly;
backs of hands are facing in opposite
directions

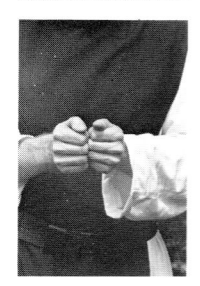

fasting

press lips together with sides of right
thumb and forefinger

fat
puff up cheeks and hold them this way for a short time

fence
spread fingers of both hands and lay them over each other like a screen

fight
hold fists up in front of chest as though protecting oneself; left fist forward with right held back toward body; left foot is also forward

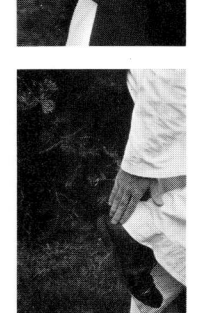

fill
move right hand horizontally at eye level from left to right; edge of hand forward

finish
hold fists together with forefingers extended, then tap tips of forefingers several times without separating hands

fish
move right hand forward in a zig-zag motion with palm facing left

fly
twist tip of right thumb at side of right mouth with other fingers spread

foot
strike right heel with palm of right hand

forget (to)
pass curved right forefinger across bridge of nose

fork

move three fingers of right hand forward; palm up and other fingers held firmly down by thumb

friend

curve fingers of both hands and then hook them together; back of right hand is up and back of left down

fruit

strike left elbow with palm of right hand; left forearm is vertical with hand closed

front

strike stomach with palm of right hand

G

gloves

hold out left hand with fingers pointing up, then pass right hand down over them to wrist as though putting on a glove

grass

hold out both hands with palms facing each other, fingers held tightly against each other, then move hands up and down alternately as though chopping something

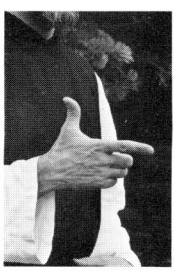

gun

point right forefinger forward from fist and raise thumb like pointing a pistol

H

hammer

with right fist make a hammering motion; heel down

happy

place tips of forefingers at respective sides of mouth, then push sides up so that the mouth's ends are pointing up slightly

hay

hold out hands with palms facing each other, heels down and fingers tightly against each other, then move hands up and down alternately as though chopping something

head

place palms of both hands on respective sides of head, then bow head a bit

hear (to)

cup right hand and place it behind right ear

high

hold right hand with palm down above head but in front of body to indicate height

hook

close right hand, palm up, then curve right forefinger to look like a hook

horse

with right hand pull imaginary hair just at hair line, and bow head slightly

hose (water)

place tips of forefingers on tips of thumbs forming circles, then draw hands apart to sides

hour

draw a circle in front of body with tip of forefinger pointing forward

I

inch

with tips of right thumb and forefinger hold tip of left thumb (middle knuckle and tip of thumb)

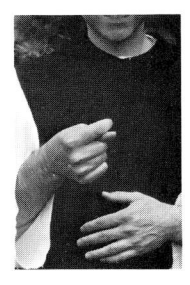

invitator
place tip of right thumb between right forefinger and middle finger; hold tightly

iron (to)
move right hand as though holding an iron and actually ironing something

K

kill (to)
place tip of right thumb under chin and move it up slightly

L

language
grasp tip of tongue with tips of right thumb and forefinger

last
throw right fist over right shoulder

leather
pinch the skin on back of left hand with tips of right forefinger and thumb

leave it
hold out hands with palms forward, then move hands slowly towards ground once or twice

like (to)
place right palm over heart then place left palm over the back of the right hand

long
touch left fist with right thumb and forefinger, then draw right hand away as though drawing on a string

M

machine
hold out fists of both hands next to each other, then twirl thumbs around each other several times

make
move fingertips of both hands down over chest in unison; palms open

me
point to chest with tip of right forefinger; tip is in contact with chest

metal
hold out left forefinger, then pass right forefinger and middle finger down over it several times as though filing a piece of metal

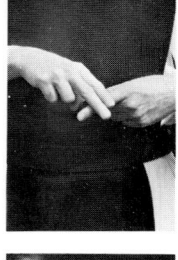

milk
hold out left forefinger from fist so that it faces left, then grasp the tip of it with tips of right forefinger, middle finger and thumb, and draw them away from left forefinger several times

minute (small)
same sign as LITTLE

money
hold out left hand with palm up, then push tip of right thumb over tip of right forefinger several times as though counting money into the left palm

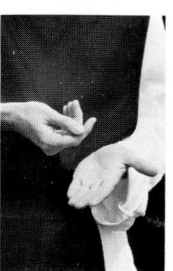

more
draw a line from shoulder to shoulder across the chest with tip of right forefinger

mother
pass right forefinger and middle finger across the forehead from left to right; fingers are pointing to the left

mule*
place tip of right thumb in right ear,
then raise and lower the fingers

N

nail
place tip of right forefinger on the
nail of vertical left forefinger

name
with tips of right forefinger, middle
finger and thumb make believe grasping a pen, then move hand as though
writing

next
push right fist forward from right
shoulder; do this only once

no
shake right hand vigorously at side of
body

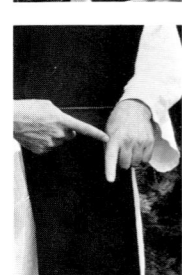
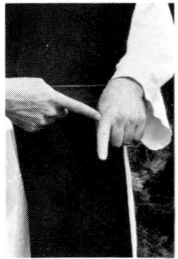

none
point to bottom of left forefinger with
right forefinger, and add sign of
OFFICE

nothing
shake right hand vigorously at side of
body

novice
place extended right forefinger and
middle finger behind right ear

now
point to the ground with tip of right
forefinger

number
spread right forefinger and middle finger from fist, then place the same configuration of the left hand over right fingers so that the symbol for number is made (#)

nun
grasp the hood next to right ear with right hand, then tug on it slightly

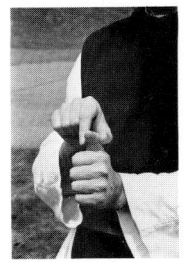

nut
hold out left thumb in vertical position with inside tip facing forward, then grasp it from behind with tips of right forefinger and thumb, right thumb on left side of left thumb

O

oblate
strike the outside of right knee with edge of right hand with palm up

old
strike left shoulder with edge of right hand several times

open
place hands back to back so that palms are facing in opposite directions, then move them apart

ordo
hold out left hand with palm down, then place right hand across back of left hand

organ
spread fingers apart and make believe playing the organ's keyboard; hands move from side to side

over
move open right hand forward in a slight arching motion; palm down

P

pail

describe a horizontal circle with tip of right forefinger, then close hand as though grasping a pail handle, then raise the hand

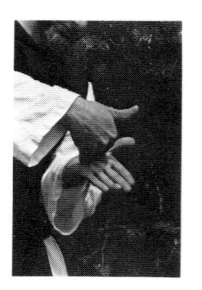

paint

hold out open left hand with palm up, then with the tips of right fingers make believe applying paint to a surface with a brush

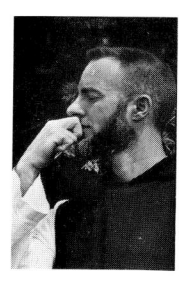

patch

strike the left forearm, elbow and biceps with the palm of the right hand in that order

pax

bring right fist to mouth and kiss knuckles of forefinger and middle finger

peace

same as PAX

peach

lightly rub right cheek with tips of right fingers; palm facing cheek

penance

move right fist from shoulder to shoulder several times as though flogging oneself with a whip

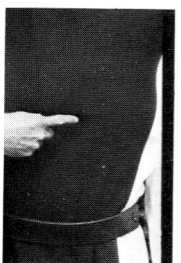

permission

trace a small circle on the stomach with tip of right forefinger

pick

curve right forefinger and extend from fist, then actually pick with it

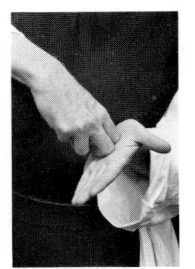

picture
curl right forefinger and middle finger, then press them into palm of left hand

pipe
place tips of thumbs and forefingers on each other forming circles, then draw them away from each other to sides

please
bring right hand to mouth and kiss tips of fingers

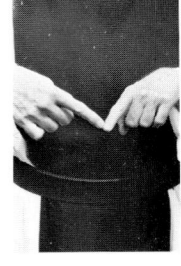

pound
hold out hands with palms up, then raise and lower them alternately

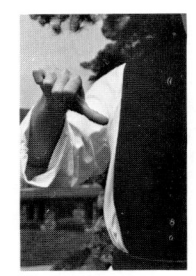

pour
close right hand with thumb extended, then slowly turn hand over sidewards as though pouring some liquid from a jug

prime*
extend left forefinger from fist in horizontal position, then place tip of right forefinger on left nail

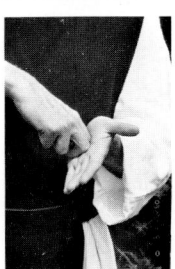

print
curl right forefinger and middle finger, then press them into palm of left hand

prostration
hold out hands side by side with palms down, then move the hands forward toward ground

pull (to)
hold out left fist before right fist, then bring them in towards the body as though pulling on a rope

push (to)
hold out hands side by side with fingers
pointing up, then push hands forward
as though pushing someone

put away (to)
place palm of right hand into left
armpit; raise left arm slightly

Q

question
draw an imaginary question mark in
the air with the tip of right forefinger

R

razor
curl right forefinger and place below
right ear, then draw it down along
right cheek as though shaving

red
place tip of right forefinger on lower
lip, then bend lip down a bit

right
hold out right hand with thumb side
up in front of right side of face, then
move hand down as though sighting
a line

ring (a)
place an imaginary ring on third finger
of left hand with tips of right forefinger
and thumb

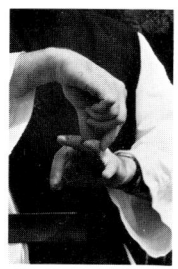

rock
strike right temple with knuckles of
right forefinger and middle finger;
hand closed

room
join the tips of the fingers of both hands
to form a roof

rubber (footwear)
grasp heel of right shoe with right forefinger and thumb

rule
hold out open left hand with fingers pointing to right, then pass tips of right fingers along outside edge of left hand

S

saint
interlace the fingers of hands and look up to heaven

salad
hold out hands with palms facing each other, then move hands up and down alternately as though chopping something

scale
hold out hands side by side with palms up, then raise and lower them alternately

screen
spread fingers of both hands and lay them over each other like a screen

separate
hold out hands next to each other with backs facing each other, then move them apart to opposite sides

sew
hold out left hand with palm down, then move right forefinger and thumb across the fingers of the left hand stopping ever so slightly at each finger as though putting a needle and thread through fingers

sext
place tip of right forefinger on middle joint of extended left forefinger and make sign for OFFICE

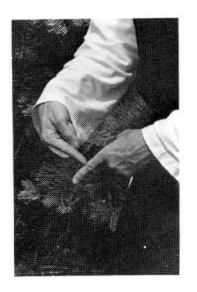

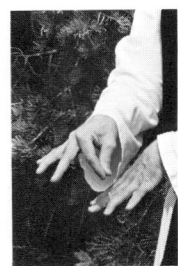

shave (to)
curl right forefinger and place beneath right ear, then draw finger down over cheek as though shaving; side of finger is on cheek

shower
join fingers of both hands in pear-shaped configuration, then point fingers down and move hands up and down alternately

shut off (to)
place tip of right thumb under chin, then raise the chin a little with thumb

sick
place right elbow into right side, then drop the forearm to the right

sign
raise both hands with palms facing chest and fingers spread wide, then wriggle fingers rapidly back and forth

sister
grasp the hood near right ear with tips of right forefinger and thumb, then tug on hood

skip it
hold out right hand with palm down, then move the hand forward in a slight arching motion

small
place tip of right little finger on right side of mouth, then turn the finger a bit

soap
rub the right cheek with the knuckles of the right fist

socks

hold the right sock with tips of right forefinger and thumb near the shoe

sorry

strike the chest with the right fist several times

stairs

hold out hands in front of body, then slowly raise them alternately as though climbing a ladder

stamp

curl forefinger and middle finger of right hand, then place the knuckles into palm of left hand

sugar

place tip of right forefinger between lips, and then purse lips as though tasting sweet sugar; a slight sucking motion with lips

sweep

hold out left hand with palm up, then pass the edge of right hand over left palm several times as though sweeping

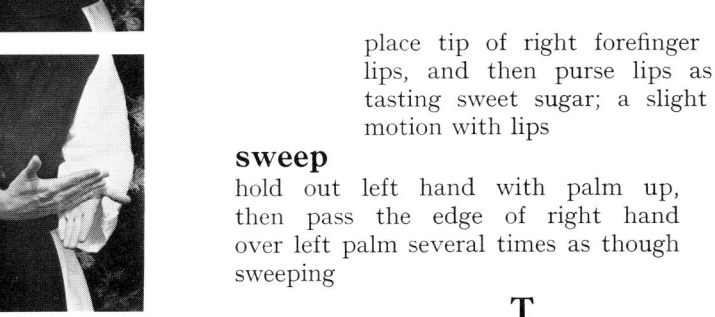

T

tea

hold up left forefinger vertically, then place middle joint of right forefinger on tip of left forefinger, forming a "T"

telephone

place right fist to right ear and hold left fist at mouth as though holding an old-fashioned telephone

tell (to)

put tip of right forefinger to mouth then move finger forward

ten wheeler (truck)
raise ten fingers, then draw a circle with right forefinger, and add sign of MACHINE

thin
hold out both hands in front of body with palms facing chest and all fingers spread wide, then pass fingers of right hand through fingers of left hand several times

this
point to the ground with tip of right forefinger

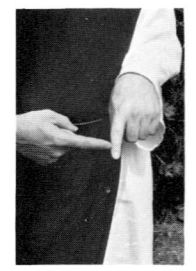

tierce
point to first joint to left forefinger with tip of right forefinger, and add sign of OFFICE

time
place closed fists side by side (thumb sides), then raise the little fingers

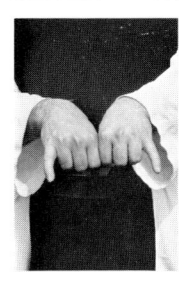

tongue
grasp tip of tongue with tips of right forefinger and thumb

typewriter
hold hands in front of body with fingers loose, then move hands up and down as though typing

U

up
hold open hands with palms up before face, then raise the hands up above head

V

vegetable
hold fingers of left hand together, then grasp them with fingers of right hand, then draw right fingers up over left fingers

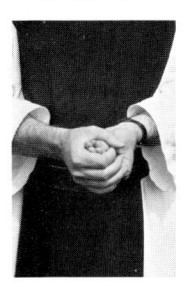

violet
place right forefinger and middle finger horizontally on forehead with fingers pointing left

vote
hold left thumb against left forefinger, then place them between a slit formed by the right thumb pressing against the other fingers of the right hand

W

wait
hold hands out before body with palms facing the ground, then move hands towards the ground a bit several times

want (to)
place left palm over heart, then place right palm over back of left hand

wax
place right forefinger sideways on mouth, then move the finger across the lips once

wet
join fingers of right hand in pear-shaped configuration; point fingers up

what
raise both hands upward and outward with palms facing up

wheel
with tip of right forefinger draw a circle in front of body

wheelbarrow*
push both fists forward next to each other as though pushing a wheelbarrow and twirl thumbs around each other as motion is made

where
raise both hands upward and outward
with palms facing up

wild
whirl the right fist next to the right
ear several times

wind
hold out right hand with edge forward,
then gently blow on the back of the
hand

window
scratch the front teeth with the tip
of the right forefinger

wrap (to)
hold hands out in front of body, then
twirl them around one another several
times

Authorized List of Signs for St. Joseph's Abbey

DERIVED SIGNS

A

afternoon
> signs of AFTER, DAY and EAT

Allen barn
> signs of A, COW and HOUSE

altar
> signs of MASS and TABLE

angel
> signs of WING and SAINT

angelus
> signs of BELL, LADY and GOD

antiphonal*
> signs of BOOK, SING and NIGHT

B

barn
> signs of COW and HOUSE

bathroom
> signs of SHAME and HOUSE

bed
> signs of SLEEP and TABLE

beer
> signs of CORN and WATER

bench
> signs of LOW and TABLE

birthday
> signs of BABY and DAY

Blessed Sacrament
> signs of GOD and BREAD

boiler room
> signs of BOIL and HOUSE

breviary*
> signs of BOOK, CHOIR RELIGIOUS, SPEAK and PRAY

broom
> signs of SWEEP and TOOL

brown
> signs of BLUE and BROTHER

bulldozer
> signs of BULL, PUSH and MACHINE

burn
> signs of TOO MUCH and FIRE

C

cabbage
> signs of HEAD and VEGETABLE

cake
> signs of SWEET and BREAD

calf
> signs of BABY and COW

candle
> signs of OIL (WAX) and LIGHT

cardboard
> signs of STRONG and PAPER

carrot
> signs of YELLOW and ROOT

chalice
> signs of MASS and VESSEL

cherry
> signs of RED and GRAIN

chocolate milk
> signs of BLACK and MILK

church
 signs of PRAY and HOUSE

coffee
 signs of BLACK and DRINK

compline
 signs of EVENING and OFFICE

confession
 signs of SPEAK and FAULT

confessor
 signs of CHOIR RELIGIOUS, HEAR and FAULTS

copper
 signs of RED and METAL

cord
 signs of BIG and THREAD

cruet
 signs of WINE, WATER and VESSEL

cup
 signs of DRINK and VESSEL

D

daughter house
 signs of BABY and HOUSE

dinner
 signs of DAY and EAT

dollar
 signs of GREEN and BACK

dormitory
 signs of SLEEP and HOUSE

dump truck
 signs of UNLOAD and MACHINE

F

field
 signs of HAY and COURTYARD

foundation
 signs of BABY and HOUSE

Friday
 signs of FISH and DAY

G

garden
 signs of VEGETABLE and COURTYARD

gasoline
 signs of OIL and FIRE

grange
 signs of G, then point to northwest

grease
 signs of THICK and OIL

H

hebdomadary
 signs of CHOIR RELIGIOUS and WEEK

holy rood guild
 signs of SEW, CHASUBLE and HOUSE

honey
 signs of WING, SWEET and BUTTER

I

ice
 signs of HARD and WATER

ice cream
 signs of HARD and MILK

infirmary
> signs of SICK and HOUSE

ink
> signs of BLACK, WATER and WRITE

J

jelly dept.
> signs of SWEET, BUTTER and HOUSE

K

kitchen
> signs of COOK and HOUSE

L

lauds
> signs of MORNING and OFFICE

laundry
> signs of WASH and HOUSE

leak
> sign of LEEK

Lent
> signs of BIG, FAST and TIME

library
> signs of BOOK and HOUSE

lock
> signs of KEY and UP; or hook right forefinger between left thumb and forefinger, left palm facing left

M

Mary
> signs GOD and WOMAN (MOTHER)

mental prayer
> place right forefinger vertically over lips and add sign of PRAY (QUIET and PRAY)

meridian
> signs of DAY and SLEEP

missal
> signs of MASS and BOOK

mixt (breakfast)
> hold out open left hand with palm down, then pass edge of right hand on it from tip of little finger to lower part of thumb

mouse
> signs of CHEESE and ANIMAL

O

oatmeal
> signs of HORSE and GRAIN

office
> signs of SING and PRAYER; if recited use signs of SPEAK and PRAYER

onion
> rub eyes with fists and add sign of VEGETABLE

P

plane
> signs of METAL and WING

pole (stake)
> touch fingertips of both hands, then raise and lower them in unison

post
> same as POLE

postulant
signs of SECULAR and NOVICE

priest
signs of CHOIR RELIGIOUS and MASS; or signs of SECULAR and MASS (if a visiting priest)

psalter
signs of PSALM and BOOK

R

read (to)
signs of BOOK, then move eyes across open hands

refectory
signs of EAT and HOUSE

refrigerator
signs of COLD and HOUSE

S

sacristy
place hands on shoulders, and add sign of HOUSE

Saturday
signs of DAY and SEVEN; or signs of MARY and DAY

sawdust
signs of SAW and DUST

scullery*
signs of VEGETABLE and HOUSE

secretary
signs of BROTHER and WRITE

sheep
signs of WOOL and ANIMAL

shovel
signs of DIG and TOOL

side
place right hand on right hip

silage*
signs of SWEET and CORN

snow
signs of WHITE and RAIN

spade
signs of DIG and TOOL

stake truck*
signs of 51, WOOD, SIDE and MACHINE

storeroom
signs of HIDE and HOUSE

Sunday
signs of GOD and DAY

supper
signs of EVENING and EAT

switch
move right hand up and down as though shutting off and turning on a wall switch

T

tractor
signs of RED and HORSE

tree
signs of GREEN and WOOD; or signs of TALL and WOOD

V

vacuum cleaner
signs of DUST and MACHINE

vespers
  signs of DAY and PRAY

vigils
  signs of NIGHT and OFFICE

vinegar
  signs of SOUR and WINE

W

wardrobe
  signs of SEW and HOUSE

wire
  signs of METAL and THREAD

Original Signs

ORIGINAL SIGNS

THE SIGNS CONTAINED in this appendix are of special significance to the members of the monastic community who find it necessary to communicate on a wider level of human social intercourse. Indeed, these signs are an attempt to make up for the deficiencies of the authorized signs, and to fill the gaps created by an inadequate vocabulary. Most of these signs are simply synonyms for words in the authorized list but they apparently take on greater meaning when contained in a phrase or compound sign particularly when that phrase or compound sign is modelled after the spoken language. Some signs then are attempts to echo the spoken language. Others are pantomimic, that is, they re-create the actual movement that one would make when performing a specific act.

As with some of the authorized signs, some original signs assign qualities or characteristics associated with persons, saints and members of the community. Members of the chapter are identified by their occupations in some instances and by their adopted names in others. This is also true of machinery; signs for these mimic the actions which they perform.

Although the moral implications of the use of these signs are important in terms of the monastic life, these signs reveal the need to communicate humor, information and emotion which would not be otherwise possible by using only authorized signs.

a

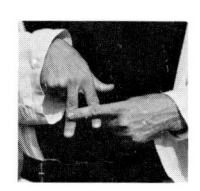

point forefinger and middle finger of left hand down with other fingers pressed into palm and back of hand facing forward, then place right forefinger across them forming an 'A' configuration

b

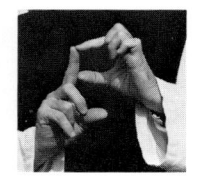

hold left forefinger vertically from fist, then place tip of right forefinger on side of tip of left and tip of thumb on side of middle joint of left forefinger; then repeat this so that tip of right forefinger is on side of middle joint of left forefinger and the tip of thumb on base of left finger.

c

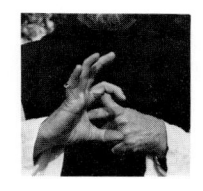

hold up left forefinger but with slight curve to it and thumb with slight curve to it (tips pointing right), then trace a 'C' from tip of forefinger to tip of thumb with right forefinger

d

hold up stiff right forefinger from fist, then place tip of left forefinger and tip of left thumb on tip of right forefinger and on lower part of right forefinger respectively

e

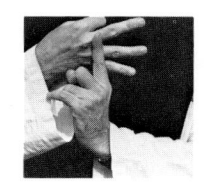

hold out first three fingers of left hand so that they point to the right, then place stiff right forefinger over them so that it is vertical; forefinger should be placed near main knuckles of left hand

f

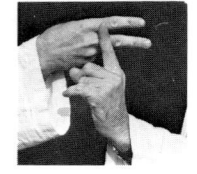

hold out first two fingers of left hand so that they point to the right, then place vertical right forefinger over them near main knuckles

g

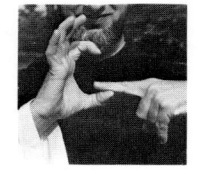

curve left forefinger and thumb so that a 'C' configuration is formed, then place tip of right forefinger on tip of thumb to complete 'G' configuration

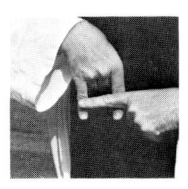

h

extend little finger and forefinger of left hand so that they point downwards, then place forefinger of right hand across them to form 'H' configuration

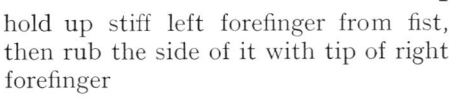

i

hold up stiff left forefinger from fist, then rub the side of it with tip of right forefinger

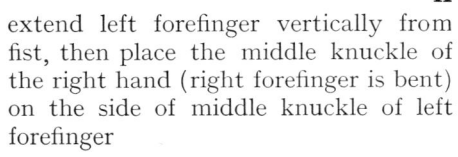

j

hold up stiff left forefinger and extend left thumb stiffly at right angle, then rub the forefinger down to the tip of the thumb with tip of the right forefinger and when tip of thumb is reached make upward sweep

k

extend left forefinger vertically from fist, then place the middle knuckle of the right hand (right forefinger is bent) on the side of middle knuckle of left forefinger

l

extend stiff left forefinger vertically and thumb at right angle to it, then from the tip of the left forefinger to the tip of the thumb draw an 'L' configuration on the inside of the forefinger and thumb with the tip of the right forefinger; when tip of left thumb is reached line should be continued straight out

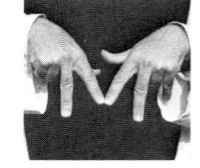

m

extend forefingers and middle fingers of both hands down so that tips of forefingers touch then spread both pairs of fingers apart so that 'M' configuration is formed; fingers pointed down

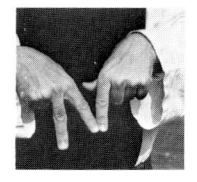

n

extend forefingers of both hands downwards and middle finger of right hand so that tips of forefingers touch forming an 'N' configuration

o

spread out fingers of right hand except forefinger and thumb which form an 'O' by touching their tips together

p

extend left forefinger vertically, then form a small circle with tips of right thumb and forefinger and place it on side of tip of left forefinger

q

form a circle with tips of left forefinger and thumb, then place tip of right forefinger slightly in bottom of this circle

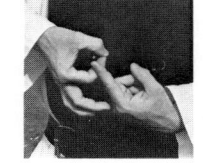

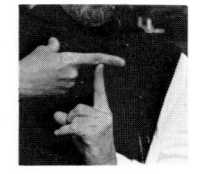

r

extend left forefinger vertically, then draw loop and tangential line with tip of right forefinger

s

form 'C' configuration with left forefinger and thumb, then trace the upper half of an 'S' on the inside surfaces of it from top of forefinger to tip of thumb and continue with second half of 'S' by sweeping forefinger beneath thumb

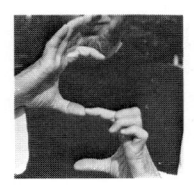

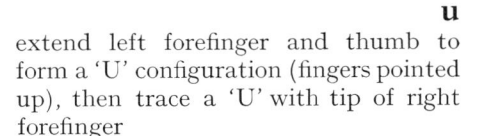

t

extend left forefinger, then place right forefinger over its tip forming a 'T' configuration

u

extend left forefinger and thumb to form a 'U' configuration (fingers pointed up), then trace a 'U' with tip of right forefinger

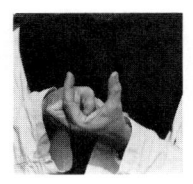

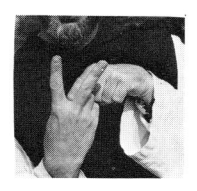

V

extend forefinger and middle finger of left hand to form 'V,' then trace it with right forefinger

extend forefingers and thumbs of both hands vertically so that tips of forefingers are touching with middle fingers spread outward

W

X

cross forefingers of both hands so that 'X' configuration is formed

make 'V' configuration with left forefinger and middle finger with back of hand forward, then place tip of right forefinger between main knuckles of forefinger and middle finger so that 'Y' configuration is formed

y

Z

extend left forefinger facing right, then place tip of right middle finger on the main knuckle of left forefinger and extend right forefinger forming a 'Z' configuration

A

above

signs of OVER + HEAD; OVER + TOP

Abraham

signs of NUMBER + ONE + JEW + A

across

sign of OPPOSITE

Adam

signs of NUMBER + ONE + SECULAR

addition

signs of number to be added + sign of PLUS + signs of number to be added + sign of EQUAL + signs of sum; ex: 1 PLUS 2 EQUAL 3

advice

signs of GIVE + RULE (directions); GIVE + TEACH; GIVE + SPIRITUAL + HELP (spiritual advice)

Africa

signs of BLACK + COURTYARD

afternoon

signs of AFTER + DAY + EAT

against

turn body to one side and add sign of WALL

agitate (to)

sign of CONFUSED

agree (to)

sign of GEAR

air

blow on back of right hand

airplane

signs of WING + MACHINE

ale

sign of BEER

all

can be used as COMMON; ex: COMMON + HOUSE

allow (to)

signs of PERMIT

all shook up

signs of ALL + SHAKE + UP

alms

hold out right hand with palm up and slightly closed

all right

signs of ALL + WRITE

always

signs of ALL + TIME

and

signs of ALL + SAME; ALL + SEW; ON + OTHER + HAND

Andrew

signs of ROCK + SAINT + SECULAR + BROTHER

anoint (to)

sign of OIL + draw a cross on palm

another

signs of ONE + MORE

anybody

sign of ANYONE

anyone

signs of ALL + ONE; can also apply to ANYTHING

apple cider
> signs of APPLE + SIDE + R

arrange (to)
> sign of MAKE (to); can be applied to any action requiring organization; ex: ARRANGE + TABLE; ARRANGE + MEETING

as a result
> sign of THUS

as far as
> signs of EQUAL + LONG + UP + TWO

Ash Wednesday
> signs of DUST + DAY; in this context DUST means to sprinkle dust on head

ask (to)
> make question-mark in air with tip of right forefinger

assist (to)
> sign of HELP

Assumption
> signs of LADY + GOD + UP

as well as
> signs of ALL + SEW + point to object + CLOSE + TWO + SAME

at
> signs of CLOSE + TWO

Australian
> signs of DOWN + UNDER

average
> sign of ABOUT

B

Babylon
> signs of OLD + BAD + TALK + SECULAR + COURTYARD

back to the old grind
> signs of BACK + TWO + OLD + GRIND

back up (to)
> signs of BACK + UP

ball
> form hands as though holding a ball

baloney
> signs of BULL + O + KNEE; BULL + LOW + KNEE

ban (to)
> signs of UNDER + BLACK + PAPER (LIST)

bandage
> sign of PATCH

bandage (to)
> signs of PATCH + UP

bathroom
> signs of SHAME + HOUSE

battery
> signs of FIRE + BOX

beat (to)
> make believe beating someone with both fists but with the heels of them so that hands come down at an angle

beer
> signs of CORN + WATER

bet

sign of MONEY

bet (to)

signs of GIVE + MONEY

big dipper

signs of BIG + DIP + R

begin (to)

signs of GO + NOW; ARRANGE + NOW; RIGHT + NOW + GO

behind

signs of B + BACKSIDE

bellicose

sign of WILD

below

sign of UNDER

bend

make believe one is bending a bar with both hands

bend over (to)

bow body slightly forward + sign of OVER

beneath

sign of UNDER

Benedictines

signs of BLACK + MONK

berries

sign of GRAIN

beside

signs of B + SIDE

besides

signs of B + SIDE

Bethlehem

signs of SECULAR + COURTYARD + BABY + GOD + COME

Bethsheba

signs of BEAUTIFUL + LADY + MARRY + PSALM + KING

between

signs of HALF + WAY

bid (to)

signs of I + GIVE + SEW + MUCH; I + ASK + HOW + MUCH; HOW + MUCH + ASK + FOUR

big deal

signs of BIG + SPREAD

bite (to)

move jaws as though biting on something

bleed (to)

signs of RED + WATER + COME; UNLOAD + MUCH + RED + WATER

blood

signs of RED + WATER

blow (to)

blow out very hard from mouth as though extinguishing a flame

blow out

signs of BLOW

blue

signs of LADY + GOD + PAINT

Boston

signs of B + COURTYARD

brake
   signs of BREAK

break (to)
   can be applied to anything torn, out of order, broken, to take a break, break even

breed (to)
   sign of MARRIAGE

brown
   signs of BROTHER + PAINT

brush (to)
   rub right palm on back of left hand

build (to)
   signs of ARRANGE + UP

but
   signs of ALL + SAME

by
   signs of B + SIDE

C

cabinets
   sign of BATHROOM

Caesar
   signs of NUMBER + ONE + SOLDIER + KING + POPE + COURTYARD

Cain
   signs of NUMBER + ONE + LITTLE + SECULAR + KILL + BROTHER

call (to)
   cup hands around mouth as though calling out

Calvary
   signs of CROSS + MOUNTAIN

camera
   hold hands at face as though holding a box camera then press down right forefinger as though pressing a shutter button

Canada
   signs of BIG + C + COURTYARD + point to north

cast (to)
   sign of THROW; make gesture like casting a fishing line with a rod

catch (to)
   sign of TAKE

Catholic
   signs of MAKE + SIGN OF CROSS (on chest)

cement
   sign of SOUP; used when cement is semi-solid

cereal
   sign of GRAIN

Ceylon
   signs of C + LONG

chain saw
   signs of WORK + PULL + CHAIN + SAW

chance
   sign of PICK

change
   sign of UNLOAD

chat (to)

sign of DIALOGUE except one hand is used; also applied to TALKS TOO MUCH

choice

signs of TAKE + PICK

chop (to)

move right hand up and down as though chopping something with edge of hand

Christmas

signs of BABY + GOD + DAY

cinema

hold left hand in front of face as though looking through a view-finder then move right hand in circular motion at side of face as though grinding

Cincinnati

signs of SIN + SIN + A + T

Citeaux

signs of SEE + TOE

city

signs of SECULAR + COURTYARD; implication of this sign is really WORLD or any large area outside of monastery

class

sign of TEACH

cloak

sign of COAT + cross arms over one another on chest but loosely

clothes

grasp fabric with tips of right forefinger and thumb and rub all together

cobbler

signs of SHOE + HOUSE

coffee

signs of BLACK + WATER; BLACK + DRINK

cold (sniffles)

rub forefinger and thumb on nostrils then on to chest and make believe wiping them on chest

color

sign of PAINT

common

sign of ALL

computer

signs of I + B + M

confessor

signs of HEAR + FAULT

consequently

sign of THUS

constitution (of Order)

signs of ALL + RULE + BOOK

contain (to)

signs of HIDE + UNDER

contempt

brush tips of right fingers from throat up to chin then out quickly with back of hand forward

cord

signs of BIG + THREAD

cost

signs of HOW + MUCH + MONEY; HOW + MUCH + MONEY + YOU + THINK

count (to)

hold out left hand then touch tips with right forefinger as though counting

courtyard

applied to any large area, city, parking lot, field, garden

cream

signs of TOP + MILK; THICK + MILK

creep (to)

sign of SNAKE

cry (to)

rub knuckles of both hands on eyes or lower eyelids

cut (to)

see WOUND

Czech

sign of CHECK MARK

Czechoslovakia

signs of CHECK + COURTYARD

D

dairyman

sign of FARMER

Dakota

signs of D + COAT + A

dark

signs of MUCH + BLACK; used to refer to colors such as DARK RED

dark red

signs of MUCH + BLACK + RED

daughter

signs of WOMAN + ME + CHILD + SECULAR

David (king)

signs of KING + SAINT; PSALM + KING; DAY + V

day after tomorrow

sign of TOMORROW two times

deal

sign of SPREAD

decide (to)

signs of D + SIDE; ARRANGE + HEAD + BEFORE + TIME

deer

place thumbs on temples and spread other fingers widely

desert

signs of DRY + SAND + COURTYARD

devil

hit forehead with tip of right forefinger or fist several times moving it from one side to other

devote (to)

sign of D then, make a circle with tips of left forefinger and thumb into circle

dialogue

signs of DIE + A + WOOD; also like TALK except two hands are used and thumbs are hit rapidly against other fingers

die (to)

signs of GO + DEAD

dip (to)
make a motion with right hand as though dipping a ladle into soup

discuss (to)
signs of SPEAK + ABOUT

Dominicans
signs of O + P (ORDER OF PREACHERS)

downstairs
signs of DOWN + STAIRS

draw (to)
make believe drawing a picture with right hand

draw towards (to)
move arms towards body as though drawing an object towards one

drive (to)
with both arms make a motion as though holding a steering wheel and driving a car

dump truck
signs of LOAD + MACHINE

Dutch
signs of HOUSE + ARRANGE + CORN + WATER

E

early
sign of QUICK

earn (to)
signs of ARRANGE + MUCH + MONEY; WORK + FOUR; TAKE + MONEY

east
sign of E + point to direction

Easter
sign of GOD + UP + DAY; EGG + DAY

Egypt
signs of DRY + SAND + COURT-YARD + ARRANGE + PYRAMID

electrician
signs of BROTHER + CHARGE + LIGHT

Elizabeth
signs of SECULAR + LADY + JOHN THE BAPTIST

employ
signs of WORK; GIVE + WORK

England
signs of E + TONGUE + COURT-YARD; DRINK + T + COURTYARD

English
sign of BISCUIT (bite middle knuckle of right forefinger)

Epiphany
signs of THREE + KING + DAY; E + P + PHONE + E; E + P + PHONE + Y

equipment (tools)
drop right hand down several times in front of body (back of hand downwards)

Esau
>   signs of E + SAW

Eve
>   signs of NUMBER + ONE + SECULAR + LADY

everybody
>   sign of EVERYONE

everyone
>   signs of ALL + ONE

everywhere
>   signs of ALL + AROUND

excuse
>   sign of FAULT

experience
>   signs of REALLY + HIT + ME

extra grace
>   signs of BIG + OIL

F

fail (to)
>   signs of NO + GO; extend thumb from fist then turn it over so that thumb points down

Fall (Autumn)
>   signs of END + HOT + TIME; a qualifying phrase is usually added for clarity

family
>   sign of SECULAR

farmer
>   signs of WORK + HAY + COURTYARD; CHARGE + ANIMALS (name animals where possible)

feed (to)
>   signs of GIVE + EAT

feel (to)
>   make motion with right hand as though feeling for something + AROUND + YOU

female
>   sign of LADY

filler
>   signs of FILL + R; this machine used in production of preserves

fix shoe (to)
>   signs of ARRANGE + SKIN

flea
>   signs of LITTLE + BIRD + ANIMAL; LITTLE + SCRATCH + ANIMAL

flee (to)
>   signs of GO + FLY + QUICK; RUN + BEFORE

flour
>   sign of GRAIN

flour
>   sign of FLOWER; WHITE + FLOWER + FOUR + COOK; GRAIN + FLOWER

flu
>   sign of FLY

for
>   sign of FOUR

forgive (to)
>   signs of FOUR + GIVE

France
>   signs of F + TONGUE + COURTYARD

freeze (to)
> signs of ARRANGE + TWO + COME + COLD; ARRANGE + HARD + WATER

freezer
> signs of HIDE + COLD + HOUSE

frequently
> sign of USUALLY

Friday
> signs of FISH + DAY

furnace
> signs of FIRE + BOX

G

Gabriel
> signs of WING + SAINT + G

Galilee
> signs of SECULAR + COURTYARD + CROSS + GOD

garage
> sign of MACHINE SHOP

gasoline
> signs of FIRE + WATER

gears
> spread fingers of both hands so that they face each other, then place them in between each other and turn the hands so that fingers intermesh; do this several times

German
> with tips of thumbs and forefingers of both hands twist them as though turning a moustache at sides of mouth

Germany
> sign of GERMAN; applied to anything German

get rid of (to)
> sign of UNLOAD

Gethsemane
> signs of FLOWER + COURTYARD + CROSS + GOD + PRAY

glass
> scratch front teeth with tip of right fingernail

go jump in the lake
> signs of PLEASE + GO + DIVE + WATER + COURTYARD

gold
> signs of YELLOW + METAL

goodbye
> hold up right hand with palm forward, then shake it from side to side several times

good-day
> signs of GOOD + DAY

good deal
> signs of GOOD + SPREAD

Good Friday
> signs of GOOD + FISH + DAY

good morning
> signs of GOOD + MORNING

grace
> signs of BLESSING + PRAYER (before eating); THANK + PRAYER (after eating)

grace
    sign of OIL

grain
    sign of BERRY; also used for cereal, flour

grapevine
    signs of WINE + FRUIT + WOOD

grind (to)
    with right hand make motion like turning a drum of a grinding machine, but motion is first over then under

groundskeeper
    signs of RELIGIOUS + CHARGE + FLOWER

grow (to)
    signs of MAKE + BIG; ARRANGE + VEGETABLE + TWO + COME + UP

guitar
    with right hand make motion like strumming a guitar's strings

H

haircut
    sign of SCISSORS at top of head; CUT + touch hair at top of head

hang (to)
    drop head to one side, then hold hands at side of neck as though holding a rope

happy
    smile, then place tip of right forefinger on side of mouth

hardship
    signs of HARD + SHIP

hat
    sign of CALOTTE

have (to)
    sign of TAKE (to)

Hawaii
    signs of HIGH + Y + E

hear (to)
    cup right hand behind right ear or put right little fingertip in ear

heat
    blow on open left hand

heaven
    signs of GOD + COURTYARD

hell
    sign of DEVIL; L

help (to)
    sign of SAVE (someone)

hermit
    signs of DIRT + ABBOT

hit (to)
    hit closed left fist into right palm

hold (to)
    tighten fists + STRONG

holy day
    signs of BIG + USELESS + DAY; SAINT + DAY; NO + WORK + DAY

hope (to)
    signs of PRAY + FOUR

horse around (to)
    signs of HORSE + AROUND

hot dog
signs of HOT + DOG; also used as exclamation

however
sign of MOREOVER

hurricane
signs of QUICK (HURRY) + CANE

hurt (to)
sign of PENANCE, DISCIPLINE, PAIN; signs of MUCH + SICK

hurt one (to)
signs of YOU + GIVE + ME + PAIN

I

ice
signs of HARD + WATER

Iceland
signs of ICE + COURTYARD

idle
sign of USELESS

in
sign of UNDER

in back of
place hand on lower part of back

Indian ocean
signs of BIG + WATER + INDIAN

indulgence
sign of PERMISSION

in front of
place palm on chest; signs of GO + BEFORE

- - ing forms
add letter N to root sign; ex: I + COME + N; this also applied to —EN forms; ex: HARD + N

in good health
signs of MUCH + STRONG; STRONG + EQUAL + BULL

in the middle of
signs of HALF + HALF; BETWEEN

inside
sign of UNDER

intelligent
signs of VERY + SMART

into
sign of UNDER

invite (to)
signs of ASK + TWO + COME

Iowa
signs of EYE + O + A

Ireland
signs of GREEN + COURTYARD

Irish
sign of GREEN; POTATO + EAT

J

Jerusalem
signs of NUMBER + ONE + JEW + SECULAR + COURTYARD + J

Jesuits
signs of S + J (Society of Jesus)

Jew

place heel of right hand on chin and tips of fingers on teeth then move fingers back and forth several times as though playing Jew's Harp

jewelry

specify color of stones + BEAUTI- FUL + ROCKS

Job

signs of OLD + GOD + BOOK + SECULAR + CRY + TOP + MANURE + PILE

Joel

signs of OLD + GOD + BOOK + TEACHER + J + O + L

John the Baptist

signs of BLESS + WATER + OUR + SAINT + J

John the Evangelist

signs of SAINT + WRITE + NUMBER + FOUR + GOD + BOOK

Jonah

signs of OLD + GOD + BOOK + TEACHER + BIG + FISH + EAT

Jonathan

signs of FRIEND + PSALM + KING

Jordan River

signs of WATER + ROAD + CLOSE + TWO + GOD + BOOK + COURT- YARD

Joseph (saint)

signs of WOOD + SAINT

Joseph (of Egypt)

signs of OLD + WOOD + SAINT

Joshua

signs of NUMBER + ONE + SOLDIER + HELP + MOSES or M

Judah

sign of JEW

Judas

signs of SECULAR + TAKE + THREE + O + WHITE + MONEY + KILL + CROSS + GOD

Judeah

signs of AROUND + NUMBER + JEW + SECULAR + COURTYARD

K

knee

touch right knee with right hand; can be used to form adjective endings but note that first element of compound must end with –n; ex: FUN + KNEE=FUNNY; CORN + KNEE=CORNY

know (to)

place fists of both hands on sides of head

L

labeller

signs of STAMP + MACHINE

lake

signs of WATER + COURTYARD

language

sign of TONGUE

late

with tip of right forefinger scratch between eyebrows several times

later today
> signs of LATE + NOW + DAY;
> LATE + R + NOW + DAY

laundry
> signs of WASH + HOUSE

lawn
> signs of GREEN + HAY

lay down (to)
> signs of GIVE + DOWN + point to
> place; PUT + DOWN + point to
> place

Lazarus
> signs of SECULAR + RAISE +
> AFTER + DEAD + FOUR + DAY

lead (to)
> signs of YOU + GO + BEFORE;
> also make motion like holding a
> horse's halter

Lebanon
> signs of MOUNTAIN + TOP + JEW
> + COURTYARD + L

lend (to)
> signs of GIVE + FOUR + LITTLE +
> TIME; JUST + LITTLE

Lent
> signs of BIG + FAST + TIME

let (to)
> signs of PLEASURE + GIVE; PLEASE
> + GIVE + INDULGENCE

letter
> make believe placing a letter in
> an envelope

lie
> sign of LIE

lie (to)
> signs of NO + TELL + RIGHT;
> ARRANGE + ERROR (MISTAKE)

light
> blow on tip of right forefinger
> then hold it up to ceiling

light (adj.)
> signs of NOT + MUCH + HEAVY

light (to)
> signs of LIGHT + UP

literature
> signs of READ + ALL + BEAUTIFUL
> + WRITING

Little Dipper
> signs of LITTLE + DIP + R

Los Angeles
> signs of L + A

love
> sign of WANT

love (to)
> sign of WANT

luck
> signs of HORSE + SHOE

Luke
> signs of SAINT + WRITE + NUMBER
> + THREE + GOD + BOOK

lumberman
> signs of CUT + WOOD; WORK +
> WOOD

M

machine shop
> signs of MACHINE + HOUSE

mail
> sign of LETTER

mail (to)
> sign of LETTER

make (to)
> sign of ARRANGE

male
> sign of BULL

Mark (saint)
> signs of SAINT + WRITE + NUMBER + TWO + CROSS + GOD + BOOK

marriage
> sign of WIFE

martyr
> signs of RED + SAINT

matins
> signs of NIGHT + SING

Matthew (saint)
> signs of SAINT + WRITE + NUMBER + ONE + CROSS + GOD + BOOK

meet (to)
> make an imaginary handshake with right hand

Melchizedek
> signs of OLD + KING + OFFER + BREAD + WINE

method
> sign of RULE

Michael (saint)
> signs of STRONG + WING + SAINT + M

Milwaukee
> signs of MILK + WALK + KEY

mimeograph machine
> with right hand make a circular motion like turning the drum of a mimeo-machine; motion is under and over

mirror
> signs of LOOK + GLASS

Miriam
> signs of SISTER + M + SING + AFTER + GO + OVER + RED + WATER

mistletoe
> signs of MASS + BOOK + TOE

mix (to)
> move hands around each other in front of body

monastery
> signs of MONK + HOUSE

Monday
> signs of WASH + DAY; DAY + TWO (FERIA SECUNDA)

monkey
> signs of MONK + KEY

months
> signs of months are made by using the number of the month or first letter of the month; context is extremely important

moon
> signs of BIG + NIGHT + LIGHT

moreover
> signs of MUCH + OVER

morning
> signs of BEFORE + DAY + EAT

Moses
> signs of NUMBER + ONE + JEW + WRITE + OLD + GOD + BOOK + M

motor
> sign of MACHINE

mountain
> make a motion as though describing mountain with hands

Mount of Olives
> signs of OIL + FRUIT + MOUNTAIN

Mount Sinai
> signs of MOUNTAIN + WRITE + TEN + TEACH

mow (to)
> push hands in front of body as though holding and pushing a lawnmower

multiplication (sign)
> cross two forefingers so that an x is formed

multiplication
> signs of number to be multiplied + sign of TIMES + sign of number to be multiplied + sign of EQUAL + number; ex: 3 x 4 = 12

mustard
> signs of HOT + DOG + BUTTER

N

narrow
> hold out hands with palms facing each other then bring them close together several times as they are pushed forward

Nazareth
> signs of SECULAR + COURTYARD + CROSS + GOD + HIDE + THREE + ZERO + YEAR

near
> signs of CLOSE + TWO; CLOSE + TWO + HAND

need (to)
> signs of LIKE + MUCH

neglect (to)
> signs of NOT + THINK + ABOUT; OVER + LOOK; FORGET + ABOUT; OVER + SEE

negro
> signs of BLACK; BLACK + SECULAR

never
> signs of NO + TIME; NOT + ONE + TIME

new
> sign of BABY; GREEN; ex: new machine: BABY + MACHINE or GREEN + MACHINE

news
> place hands near mouth with fingers facing each other then tap thumbs against other finger tips several times

New Testament
> signs of CROSS + GOD + BOOK

New York

signs of N + Y

next Sunday

signs of NEXT + GOD + DAY

no

shake right hand loosely at side several times

Noah

signs of OLD + SAINT + ARRANGE + BIG + BOAT + TIME + BIG + WATER + FILL + COME

nobody

sign of NO ONE

no one

signs of NO + ONE

north

sign of N + point to direction with forefinger

not

sign of NO

not very new

signs of NOT + MUCH + BABY

nothing

sign of ZERO; also exaggerated shaking of hand

numbers (cardinal)

use the same system as with ordinal numbers except do not use sign of NUMBER

numbers (ordinal)

to make these numbers place before number the sign of NUMBER and after the digit add sign of BEFORE, but this only for FIRST in series

ex: First: signs of NUMBER + ONE + BEFORE + point to object
Second: signs of NUMBER + TWO + AFTER + point to first object in series
Third: signs of NUMBER + THREE + AFTER + point to second object in series

O

oblate

hit side of right knee with palm of right hand

office (place)

signs of WORK + HOUSE; LITTLE + HOUSE

often

sign of USUALLY

oh dear

signs of O + DEER

Ohio

signs of O + HIGH + O

oh my

signs of O + ME

oh well

signs of O + WATER + DEEP (WELL)

old

with the edge of right hand hit left shoulder several times

Old Testament

signs of OLD + GOD + BOOK

olive

signs of OIL + FRUIT

on
> sign of TOP

on top of
> sign of TOP

opposite
> signs of ON + OTHER + SIDE; ON + NEXT + SIDE; also hold right hand vertically with palm facing chest then drop the hand so that the palm is up

orange (color)
> signs of RED + YELLOW

orchard
> signs of FRUIT + WOOD

Our Lady
> signs of GOD + MOTHER; LADY + GOD

out of (go)
> signs of GO + OUT + DOOR

outside
> point to distance with right forefinger

P

Pacific Ocean
> signs of BIG + ALL + PEACE + WATER

pagan
> signs of SECULAR + NOT + KNOW + RIGHT + GOD

pagan god
> signs of SECULAR + GOD

pall
> make a motion as though removing the cover from chalice with right hand, steadying base of chalice with left

parts of body
> must point to them in most instances

party
> signs of WILD + TIME

patch
> place right palm over left forearm in several places

Paul
> signs of SAINT + P + ALL; signs of SAINT + PALL

pay (to)
> signs of MONEY; GIVE + MONEY

peach
> rub tips of right fingers in circular motion on right cheek

penny
> signs of RED + MONEY

Pentecost
> signs of WING + GOD + DAY

permit
> sign of INDULGENCE

permit (to)
> signs of GIVE + INDULGENCE

persuade (to)
> signs of CHANGE + YOU + HEAD

Pharoah
> signs of KING + ARRANGE + OLD + JEW + SECULAR + WORK + MUCH + HARD

Philip
> signs of FILL + UP

phoney
> signs of PHONE + E; PHONE + KNEE; PHONE + Y

phonograph
> signs of PLATE + MACHINE; DISC + MACHINE

photography
> sign of CAMERA

pickaxe
> signs of PICK + CHOP + TOOL

picnic
> signs of OUT + SIDE + EAT

Pilate
> signs of SECULAR + SOLDIER + KILL + CROSS + GOD

pipe down
> make believe holding a pipe at mouth then press down tip of forefinger in the pipe's bowl (DOWN) PIPE (lead) + DOWN

place
> must name it

plan
> signs of ARRANGE + HEAD

plan (to)
> signs of ARRANGE + THINK

planet
> first letter of planet's name + LIGHT; or spell out planet's name

play (to)
> hold and move hands like playing a piano

please
> kiss inside of tips of right forefingers

plus sign
> cross forefingers to form +

pocket
> place right hand in pocket

poetry
> POUR + TREE

Poland
> signs of POLE + COURTYARD

Polish
> move extended right fist in circular motion

pop-corn
> signs of POP + CORN

porter
> signs of BROTHER + CHARGE + KEY + HOUSE; BROTHER + CHARGE + GATE + HOUSE

postulant
> signs of SECULAR + NOVICE

prepare (to)
> sign of ARRANGE

privilege
> signs of TOP + SENIORITY

problem
> draw an imaginary question-mark in the air with right forefinger

procedure
> sign of RULE

promise (to)
> signs of SWEAR + HELP + ME + GOD; SEW + HELP + ME + GOD

pronouns (possessive)
> sign of I = MINE
> sign of YOU = YOURS
> point to person = HIS, HERS
> signs of YOU + ME = OURS
> point to persons = THEIRS

pronouns (object forms)
> sign of I = ME
> sign of YOU = YOU
> point to person = HIM, HER, IT
> sign of YOU + I = US
> point to persons = THEM

pronouns (subject forms)
> sign of I = I
> sign of YOU = YOU
> point to person = HE, SHE, IT
> signs of I + YOU = WE
> signs of ALL + YOU = YOU (plural)
> point to persons = THEY

prophet
> sign of TEACHER

Protestant
> signs of NOT + SAME + SIGN OF CROSS

psalter
> signs of SALT + R

psalter (psalms)
> make believe holding and playing a flute with tip of right thumb placed on mouth and other fingers extended and moving

pull (to)
> make believe pulling on the starter cord of a machine

pump
> make motion as though pushing down on the arm of a hand pump

pumpernickle
> signs of PUMP + R + FIVE + CENTS

put (to)
> sign to ARRANGE (to); ARRANGE + THERE

pyramid
> describe a pyramid with both hands brought down sharply at angles

Q

quality control
> signs of CHECK + OVER + SWEET

quantity
> signs of BIG + NUMBER

queen
> signs of LADY + KING

queen bee
> signs of LADY + KING + SWEET + WING (BEE)

question words
> sign of Y = WHY
> signs of WHAT + TIME = WHEN
> signs of WHAT + ONE = WHO
> signs of Y = HOW; HOW + COME; WHAT + RULE
> sign of WHAT = WHAT

quit (to)
> signs of GIVE + UP; GIVE + UP + BOAT

R

Rachel
> signs of SECULAR + LADY + CRY + TIME + ALL + BABY + COME + DEAD

raise (to)
> hold out both hands at about shoulder level then raise them with palms up

rarely
> signs of NOT + MUCH

read (to)
> sign of BOOK then move head back and forth as though scanning the text

recreation
> signs of TAKE + BREAK

Red Indian
> place right hand in back of head with first two fingers extended then with left hand placed over mouth and taken away several times as though crying war whoop

Red Sea
> signs of RED + WATER + COURT-YARD

refuse (to)
> signs of TURN + UP + YOU + NOSE

remember
> signs of THINK + ABOUT; NOT + FORGET + ABOUT

research
> signs of LOOK + UP; DIG + DOWN

restaurant
> signs of SECULAR + EAT + HOUSE

retreat
> signs of PRAY + WEEK

rice
> signs of CHINESE + EAT

rich
> signs of MUCH + MONEY

rid (to)
> sign of UNLOAD

ring
> sign of MARRIAGE

ring (to)
> signs of ARRANGE + BELL

rise (to)
> sign of UP

river
> signs of WATER + ROAD

robber
> signs of DIRT + CROZIER

rule
> sign applied to anything and how done such as a skill, method, procedure, technique

run (to)

make running motion with body; also applies to operation of machine: WORK + MACHINE

Russia

signs of RED + COURTYARD

Russian

sign of RED

S

sad

signs of ALL + BREAK + DOWN; CRY

saint

sign can be placed in initial or final position

salad

signs of GREEN + HAY

salad oil

sign of OIL

Samson

signs of OLD + STRONG + JEW + COME + WEAK + AFTER + LADY + CUT + HAIR

Samuel

signs of OLD + TEACHER + ANOINT + PSALM + KING

sand

signs of LITTLE + YELLOW + DIRT

Santa Barbara

signs of SAINT + BAR + BAR + A

Saturday

signs of OUR LADY + DAY

Saul (king)

signs of KING + S + ALL; NUMBER + ONE + JEW + KING

save (to)

signs of HIDE + MONEY; HIDE + FOUR + RAIN + Y + DAY

save (to), (someone)

sign of HELP

saw (to)

pass right forefinger over left wrist with sawing motion

say (to)

sign of SPEAK

screen

sign of FENCE

secretary

sign of WRITE

secular

sign is usually applied to anything, or anybody outside of monastery as a qualifying word

sell (to)

sign of MONEY

send (to)

signs of TAKE + OVER

seniority

make a series of chopping motions with the right hand moving from side to side as though counting objects set in series

sermon

sign of TEACH

set (to)
> signs of ARRANGE + STRONG; ARRANGE + CORRECT

shake (to)
> with both hands make believe shaking someone

shave (to)
> sign of RAZOR

shed (to)
> signs of GIVE + LIGHT; ARRANGE + LIGHT + TWO + COME

shine (to)
> signs of BRUSH + UP

shiny
> signs of SHINE + KNEE; SHINE + Y; SHINE + E

ship
> sign of BOAT

ship (to)
> signs of BOX + UP

side
> slide open hand down one side of the body from chest to hip

silk
> hold tips of right forefinger and thumb near mouth, then draw them away as though drawing out a thin fibre from clenched teeth

silk screen
> signs of SILK + SCREEN

sin
> sign of FAULT; FALSE

since
> sign of FOUR

sing (to)
> sign applied to anything which makes noise

sing louder
> signs of GIVE + MORE + SPEAK (SING)

sink (to)
> signs of S + INK

sister
> sign of NUN

skill
> sign of RULE

slay (to)
> sign of DIE; DEAD; also run tip of right forefinger along throat from left to right; also hold tip of right forefinger to temple as though holding a gun to it

slit (to)
> run tip of right forefinger along throat as though cutting it; also make a vertical line with tip of right forefinger from near face down to about waist level

smart
> tap temples with tips of forefingers; sign of THINK

smoke
> signs of BLACK + AIR

smoke (to)
> hold tips of right forefinger and middle finger near mouth as though holding a cigarette

snore (to)
sign of SAW + WOOD

snoring
sign of SAW + WOOD

snow
signs of WHITE + RAIN

so
sign of SEW

soda
signs of SOFT + DRINK

Sodom
signs of BAD + SECULAR + COURT-YARD + BURN + TIME + LADY + CHANGE + TWO + SALT

soft drink
signs of SOFT + DRINK

Solomon
signs of JEW + KING + THOUSAND + LADY + MARRIAGE

so long
signs of SEW + LONG

someone
signs of ONE + BROTHER; ONE + SECULAR

something
sign of ONE

sometimes
signs of FEW + TIME; NOT + ALL + TIME

somewhere
signs of ONE + COURTYARD

south
sign of S + point to direction with forefinger

Spain
signs of CASTENETS + COURTYARD; GUITAR + COURTYARD; S+TONGUE + COURTYARD

Spanish
make motion like playing caste-nets with hands

spend (to)
sign of MONEY

spin (to)
sign of WILD

split
sign of SEPARATE (to)

spread (to)
make believe dealing out cards from a deck; ARRANGE + ALL + OVER

spring
move hands back and forth from each other as though compressing a spring then releasing it

Spring (season)
sign of SPRING

spring (to)
sign of SPRING

stamp
sign of LABEL

stamp (to)
sign of LABEL

stamp machine

    signs of STAMP + MACHINE

star

    signs of LITTLE + NIGHT + TIME + LIGHT + point to sky with fore-finger

start (to)

    signs of GO + NOW; TURN + KEY + MOTOR (ignition); GO + A + HEAD

steal (to)

    signs of TAKE + TIME + NOT + YOU

Stephen

    signs of NUMBER + ONE + RED + SAINT

stink (to)

    signs of hold nose with thumb and forefinger + throw up hand into air with disgusted look on face; SMELL + UGLY

student

    signs of ONE + WHO + WORK + BOOK; name person or point to him + GO + TWO + BOOK + CHAPTER

study (to)

    sign of KNOW

subtraction

    sign of number + sign of UNDER + number + sign of EQUALS + number; ex: 3 UNDER 4 EQUALS 1

Summer

    signs of HOT + TIME

sun

    signs of DAY + LIGHT + point to sky (literally: FIRE UP THERE)

Sunday

    signs of GOD + DAY

support (to)

    signs of BACK + UP

surface

    sign of WALL

swear (to)

    place left hand over heart and raise right hand

swim (to)

    with arms make swimming motion

T

Tabor (Mt)

    signs of MOUNTAIN + T + CROSS + GOD + UP

tape recorder

    describe circles with both fore-fingers as though reels of tape recorder were moving + sign of MACHINE

teach (to)

    signs of GIVE + CHAPTER; shake forefinger at person

teacher

    sign of TEACH (to)

tear (to)

    hold hands in front of body next to each other, then move them in opposite directions as though tearing a piece of cloth; sign of BREAK

technique

    sign of RULE

tell (to)
> sign of SAY; SPEAK + ABOUT

thanks
> sign of PLEASE

Thanksgiving
> signs of THANK + GOD + DAY

therefore
> sign of THUS

thief
> sign of ROBBER

think (to)
> tap temples with tips of fore-fingers; KNOW

through
> sign of BETWEEN

thrust (to)
> sign of THROW; MUCH + POWER; GOOD + POWER

Thursday
> signs of FIVE + DAY (FERIA QUINTA)

thus
> signs of SEW + NOW; THAT + Y

tie (to)
> signs of TIE + UP

time
> little finger extended from hand (this is also used as a diminutive)

to
> sign of TWO

together
> sign of GEAR; ALL + TOGETHER; ALL + EQUAL + TIME

toilet
> sign of BATHROOM

too bad
> signs of TWO + BAD

top dog
> signs of TOP + DOG

top of the morning to you
> signs of TOP + MORNING + TWO + YOU

tour
> signs of WALK + AROUND + HOUSE

tractor
> signs of RED + HORSE + MACHINE

train (to)
> signs of TEACH + RULE; GIVE + RULE

treasurer
> signs of MONEY + BROTHER; BROTHER + CHARGE + MONEY

trouble
> signs of CONFESSION or PAIN

Tuesday
> signs of THREE + DAY (FERIA TERCIA)

Tyre (city)
> signs of MACHINE + WHEEL; also used for TIRE

U

unload
> signs of GET RID OF or CHANGE

upstairs
> signs of UP + STAIRS

useless
> sign of BAD

usually
> signs of CLOSE + TWO + ALL + TIME; MANY + TIME

V

voice
> signs of SPEAK + BOX

W

want (to)
> draw a heart with right forefinger; hold hands over heart, one over the other

wardrobe
> signs of SEW + HOUSE

wash
> can be applied to anything that needs cleaning, or anything that needs to be put into order

Washington (city)
> signs of W + COURTYARD; WASH + COURTYARD; PRESIDENT + COURT-YARD

waste (to)
> signs of ARRANGE + USELESS; THROW + AWAY; ARRANGE + ALL + GO + DOWN + DRAIN

watch
> signs of TIME + MACHINE

watch (to)
> place thumb side of right hand over eyebrows; signs of WATCH + CLOSE

weak
> sign of WEEK

wear (to)
> signs of ARRANGE + CLOTHES

wed (to)
> sign of MARRIAGE, HUSBAND, or WIFE

Wednesday
> signs of FOUR + DAY (FERIA QUARTA)

week
> sign of WEAK

welcome
> signs of WELL + COME

well
> signs of WATER + DEEP

west
> sign of W + point to direction

wet (to)
> sign of WATER

what are you doing ?
> signs of WHAT + YOU + WORK

what news
> signs of WHAT + DIRT

why
> sign of Y

wife

  pass tips of right forefinger and thumb over third finger of left hand as though placing a ring on it

wild

  hold right hand over right shoulder then move it around several times as though twirling a lasso; sign can be applied to anything like WILD + ANIMAL or WILD + WOOD

window

  sign of GLASS

Winter

  signs of COLD + TIME

with

  signs of CLOSE + TWO; EQUAL + TIME

wood

  sign can be used as substitute for WOULD; ex: I + WOOD + LIKE + TWO + GO

work (to)

  usually applied to manual labor but can also be used to indicate whether or not a machine works; also applied to problem-solving

work for (to)

  signs of WORK + FOUR

wormy

  signs of LITTLE + WORM + Y

worry (to)

  place right fingers on teeth then move fingers back and forth over them as though biting them

worthless

  sign of BAD, USELESS

wound

  sign of CUT

Y

you know

  sign of WHO

Z

Zeus

  signs of SECULAR + GOD + FATHER + ALL

APPENDIXES

Number System

for numbers one 1 through ten (10) use the fingers and thumbs of both hands: right hand

1: forefinger

2: forefinger + middle

3: forefinger + middle + ring finger

4: forefinger + middle + ring finger + little

5: forefinger + middle + ring finger + little + thumb

6: five fingers of right hand + left forefinger

7: five fingers of right hand + left forefinger + middle finger

8: five fingers of right hand + forefinger + middle finger + ring finger

9: five fingers of right hand + left forefinger + middle finger + ring finger + little finger

10: five fingers of right hand + five fingers of left hand

11: hold vertically both forefingers side by side

for numbers twelve (12) through nineteen (19): signs of 1 + other digits

for twenty (20) make signs of TWO + ZERO; hold signs next to each other

for numbers twenty-one (21) through twenty-nine (29) make signs of TWO + other digits

for numbers thirty (30) through ninety-nine (99) make signs of THREE + ZERO, NINE + NINE

for number fifty (50) make signs of FIVE + ZERO; or place extended right forefinger over middle knuckle of extended left forefinger and then move right over left with sawing motion + sign of 100

for one hundred (100) place tip of right forefinger in open mouth but make *no* contact

for one hundred fifty (150) make signs of HUNDRED + FIFTY

for two hundred (200) make signs of TWO + HUNDRED

for two hundred and fifty (250) make signs of TWO + HUNDRED + FIFTY

for one thousand (1000) make signs of one + T; or ONE + ZERO + ZERO + ZERO

for numbers up to ninety thousand (90,000) make signs of FIVE + T; TEN + T; and so on

for one hundred thousand (100,000) make signs of HUNDRED + T; or HUNDRED + ZERO + ZERO + ZERO

for numbers up to nine hundred thousand (900,000) make signs of NINE + HUNDRED + T; or NINE + HUNDRED + ZERO + ZERO + ZERO

for million (1,000,000) make sign of M

for numbers greater than million make signs of digits + M; ex: HUNDRED + M

Fractions

for one-quarter ($\frac{1}{4}$) touch knuckle near tip of left forefinger with tip of right forefinger with sawing motion

for one-half ($\frac{1}{2}$) touch middle knuckle of left forefinger with tip of right forefinger with sawing motion

for three-quarters ($\frac{3}{4}$) make signs of THREE + PLUS SIGN + FOUR; or THREE + OVER + FOUR

for one-third ($\frac{1}{3}$) make signs of ONE + PLUS SIGN + THREE; or ONE + OVER + THREE

for three-fifths ($\frac{3}{5}$) make signs of THREE + PLUS SIGN + FIVE; or THREE + OVER + FIVE

Division

to divide one number into another make signs of one number + INTO + other number + EQUALS + numbers

APPENDIX TWO

Saints of Importance to the Cistercians

St Albric
signs of SAINT + ALB

St Benedict
signs of BLACK + ABBOT

St Bernard
signs of WHITE + ABBOT

St Eugene
signs of HOLY + FATHER + E

St Francis of Assisi
signs of POOR + SAINT + F

St Gabriel
signs of SAINT + WING + G

St Jerome
signs of SAINT + WRITE + L + TONGUE + GOD + BOOK

St John the Baptist
signs of BLESS + HOLY + WATER + SAINT

St Joseph
signs of WOOD + SAINT

St Paul
signs of SAINT + P + ALL

St Peter
signs of SAINT + ROCK

St Raphael
signs of SAINT + WING + R

St Robert
signs of NUMBER + ONE + ABBOT + CITEAUX

St Stephen Harding
signs of SAINT + HARD + N

St Theresa
signs of LITTLE + FLOWER + CHILD

St Thomas Aquinas
signs of WING + DOCTOR (angelic doctor)

Members of Saint Joseph's Abbey, Spencer, Massachusetts
(Note: These change in many cases as the monk changes his employment)

B. Alberic
signs of BROTHER + CHARGE + DUSTING + FLOORS (in charge of house cleaning)

B. Alfred
signs of OLD + BROTHER + A + CHARGE + BOOKS (librarian)

B. Ambrose
signs of BROTHER + CHARGE + VEGETABLE + COURTYARD (farm manager)

B. Anselm
signs of BROTHER + CHARGE + T + P + WRITE (asst. director of Trappist Preserves)

B. Anthony
signs of BROTHER + A + WORK + T + P + COOK + HOUSE (works in Trappist Preserves kitchen)

B. Aquinas
signs of BROTHER + A + Q

B. Arthur
signs of BROTHER + A + CHARGE + WOODS (forester; in charge of land reclaim)

B. Augustine
signs of BROTHER + A + SUB-DEACON (sub-deacon)

B. Basil
signs of BROTHER + B + WORK + SEW + HOUSE (works in wardrobe)

B. Benedict
signs of BROTHER + BLACK + ABBOT (Saint Benedict is black abbot)

B. Bernard
signs of BROTHER + B + WHITE + ABBOT + CHARGE + T + P + HOUSE (director of Trappist Preserves)

B. Bernardo
signs of BROTHER + B + FROM + BABY + HOUSE + A (visiting brother from Argentina)

B. Bonaventure
signs of BROTHER + CHARGE + KEY + HOUSE (porter)

B. Brendan
signs of BROTHER + WORK + T + P + COOK + HOUSE (works in Trappist Preserves kitchen)

B. Bruno
signs of BROTHER + CELLARER

B. Camillus
signs of BROTHER + C + WORK + SICK + HOUSE (works in infirmary)

B. Carroll
signs of BROTHER + WORK + T + P (works in Trappist Preserves)

B. Charles

signs of BROTHER + C + WORK + T + P + CHECK + OVER + SWEET (in charge of quality control for Trappist Preserves)

B. Christopher

signs of BROTHER + WORK + T + P + COOK + HOUSE (Trappist Preserves foreman)

B. Columban

signs of BROTHER + C + WRITE + FOUR + COAT + HOUSE (secretary of the Holy Rood Guild)

B. Cyril

signs of BROTHER + WORK + MONEY + HOUSE (assistant treasurer)

B. Daniel

signs of BROTHER + CHARGE + TELEPHONE

B. David

signs of BROTHER + D + HELP + COOK + HOUSE (works in kitchen)

B. David Alan

signs of BROTHER + CHARGE + COAT + HOUSE (Guild director)

B. Dominic

signs of BROTHER + D + CHARGE + SISTER + HOUSE + HAY + COURT-YARD (director of convent farm)

B. Edward

signs of BROTHER + CHARGE + EAT + HOUSE (refectorian)

B. Edward John

signs of BROTHER + E + J

B. Ephraim

signs of BROTHER + WRITE (Abbot's secretary)

B. Eric

signs of BROTHER + SUB-MASTER OF NOVICES

B. Francis

signs of BROTHER + CHARGE + SICK + HOUSE (infirmarian)

B. Frederick

signs of BROTHER + F + WORK + MACHINE + SHOP (works in garage)

B. Gabriel

signs of BROTHER + G + WING (Saint Gabriel is wing saint)

B. Gerald

signs of BROTHER + G + CHARGE + FRUIT + WOODS (orchard director)

B. Gilbert

signs of TALL + BROTHER + G + CHARGE + WOODS (head forester)

B. Gregory

signs of BROTHER + G + CHARGE + MACHINE + HOUSE (head of machine shop)

B. James

signs of BROTHER + HELP + PAINT (helps with painting)

B. Jerome

signs of BROTHER + COOK (community cook)

B. John

signs of BROTHER + PAINT; PAINT + BROTHER (painter)

B. Justin

signs of BROTHER + CHARGE + SEW + HOUSE (wardrobe head)

B. Kevin

signs of BROTHER + K + CHARGE + SHOE + HOUSE (cobbler), BROTHER + K + CHARGE + I + B + M + MACHINE (IBM operator)

B. Lawrence

signs of BROTHER + WORK + T + P + COOK + HOUSE (works in Trappist Preserves kitchen)

B. Leo

signs of BROTHER + L + WORK + T + P + LABELLER (Trappist Preserves labeller)

B. Leonard

signs of BROTHER + L + WORK + COAT + HOUSE (works in Holy Rood Guild)

B. Matthew

signs of BROTHER + CHARGE + PIPES (plumber)

B. Norbert

signs of BROTHER + N + WORK + KEY + HOUSE (asst. porter)

B. Pascal

signs of BROTHER + CHARGE + SECULAR + HOUSE (guest master)

B. Paul

signs of BROTHER + P

B. Philip

signs of BROTHER + FILL + UP

B. Richard

signs of BROTHER + R + BOX + UP + FOUR + COAT + HOUSE (Holy Rood Guild shipper)

B. Roger

signs of BROTHER + CHARGE + LIGHT (electrician)

B. Romuald

signs of BROTHER + WORK + COAT + HOUSE (works in Guild)

B. Ronald

signs of BROTHER + COOK + SECULAR + HOUSE (cook in guest house)

B. Simon

signs of BROTHER + SUB-CELLARER

B. Stephen

signs of LITTLE + BROTHER + S + WORK + COAT + HOUSE (works in Guild)

B. Thomas

signs of BROTHER + T + WORK + MACHINE + OVER + T + P (Trappist Preserves mechanic)

B. Vincent

signs of OLD + BROTHER + V

B. William

signs of BROTHER + W + CHARGE + COOK + T + P (Trappist Preserves cook)

B. Xavier

signs of BROTHER + X

F. Anselm

signs of RELIGIOUS + CHARGE + SISTER + HOUSE (convent chaplain)

F. Basil

signs of RELIGIOUS + MASTER OF CEREMONIES

F. Bede

signs of RELIGIOUS + WORK + MASS + HOUSE (Mass secretary)

F. Bernard

signs of RELIGIOUS + WHITE + ABBOT (Saint Bernard is white abbot)

F. Bonaventure

signs of RELIGIOUS + PRESIDENT (president)

F. Eugene

signs of RELIGIOUS + CHARGE + SEW + HOUSE (wardrobe keeper)

F. George

signs of RELIGIOUS + CHARGE + FLOWERS (groundskeeper)

F. Henry

signs of RELIGIOUS + H + TEACH (theology professor)

F. John

signs of SICK + RELIGIOUS + J

F. Malachy

signs of RELIGIOUS + CHARGE + CLOAK + HOUSE (sacristan)

F. Marius

signs of RELIGIOUS + CHARGE + GIVE + PRAY + WEEK + TWO + SECULAR (retreat master)

F. Mark

signs of RELIGIOUS + DOCTOR + M (medical doctor)

F. Matthew

signs of RELIGIOUS + ARRANGE + FLOWERS (floral decorator)

F. Owen

sign of PRIOR (prior)

F. Paul

signs of RELIGIOUS + CHARGE + TAPE + MACHINE (in charge of magnetic tapes)

F. Paulinus

signs of RELIGIOUS + NOVICE + MASTER (novice master)

F. Raphael

signs of RELIGIOUS + HEAD + DOCTOR (psychologist)

F. Raymond

signs of OLD + RELIGIOUS + STAY + UNDER + SICK + HOUSE

F. Regis

signs of RELIGIOUS + CHARGE + SING (cantor)

F. Robert

sign of SUB-PRIOR

F. Thomas

sign of ABBOT

F. William

signs of RELIGIOUS + CHARGE + SILK + SCREEN (art shop director)

APPENDIX FOUR

Cistercian houses

Andes (Chile)
signs of BABY + HOUSE

Ava (Missouri)
signs of A + V + A

Azul (Argentina)
signs of BABY + HOUSE + A

Bellefontaine (France)
signs of OUR + MOTHER + HOUSE

Berryville (Virginia)
signs of BABY + HOUSE + B

Citeaux (France)
signs of MOTHER + HOUSE + ALL;
BIG + CHAPTER + HOUSE; SEE +
TOE

Clairvaux
signs of WHITE + ABBOT + HOUSE

Genesee (New York)
signs of HOUSE + ARRANGE +
BREAD

Gethsemani (Kentucky)
signs of HOUSE + ARRANGE +
CHEESE

Guadalupe (Oregon)
signs of BABY + HOUSE + O

Holy Spirit (Georgia)
signs of HOLY + GOD + WING +
HOUSE

Holy Trinity (Utah)
signs of THREE + GOD + HOUSE

St. Joseph's Abbey (Spencer)
signs of WOOD + SAINT + HOUSE

Snowmass (Colorado)
signs of WHITE + RAIN + HOUSE;
WHITE + RAIN + MASS

Vina (California)
signs of HOUSE + UNDER + WINE
+ AREA

BIBLIOGRAPHY

Since little research has been carried out on monastic sign languages, indeed on any of the sign languages, the items listed here represent nearly all the published studies. Most of the literature deals with studies of particular sign lists from various monasteries in Europe, whereas, as one will quickly note, nothing is available on sign lists or the sign languages here in the United States or in Canada. Moreover, none of the published literature presented in this bibliography study the structure of monastic sign languages as we have attempted to do here. In addition, only one author has made any attempt to comment on what these signs mean in terms of the monastic life, a point which we consider essential to any detailed study of the development of the monastic sign language.[1]

The bibliography is by no means complete in regards to monastic literature. We have listed only those items consulted during the course of this project. Van Rijnberk includes in his study of some sign lists an excellent list of references to sign lists in manuscript form and some particularly scholarly commentaries.[2] Unfortunately, many of these are not available in libraries in the United States. However, we have obtained some of them in photocopy.

Studies of secular signs and gestures are voluminous; we have noted but a few of them because they relate in some manner to our work. An excellent bibliography of items published up to 1957 may be found in Francis Hayes' article, "Gestures: A Working Bibliography."[3] Professor Hayes' work is significant because it is one of the few attempts to gather printed studies into one rather complete list. As a source for materials on gestures it is indispensable.

[1] Van Rijnberk, *Le Langage*, pp. 12–14.
[2] Van Rijnberk, *Le Langage*, pp. 161–163.
[3] Francis Hayes, "Gestures: A Working Bibliography," *Southern Folklore Quarterly*, XXI (December, 1957), 218–317.

MONASTIC LITERATURE

Books

Aungier, G. J. *A History of Antiquities of Syon Monastery in the Parish of Isleworth.* London, 1840.

Bouyer, Louis. *The Cistercian Heritage.* Westminster, Maryland, 1958.

Butler, Dom Cuthbert. *Le Monachisme Bénédictin.* Paris, 1924.

Caesarius Heisterbacensis. *Dialogus Miraculorum,* 2 vols. Ridgewood, New Jersey, 1966.

de Vogüe, Adalbert. *La Règle du Maître,* Paris, 1964.

Dubois, Louis F. *Histoire Civile, Religieuse et Littéraire de l'Abbaye de la Trappe.* Paris, 1824.

Guignard, P. *Les Monuments Primitifs de la Règle Cistercienne.* Dijon, 1878.

Knowles, Dom David, editor. *The Monastic Constitutions of Lanfranc.* New York, 1951.

———. *The Monastic Order in England.* Cambridge, England, 1940.

———. *Saints and Scholars.* Cambridge, England, 1962.

Lekai, Louis. *The White Monks.* Okauchee, Wisconsin, 1953.

Milliken, E. K. *English Monasticism Yesterday and Today.* London, 1967.

Order of Cistercians of the Strict Observance. *US de l'Ordre des Cisterciens de la Stricte Observance Précédés de la Règle de Saint Benoît, de la Charte de Charité et des Constitutions.* Westmalle, 1926.

———. *Usages of the Cistercian Monks of the Strict Observance.* Monte Cistello, 1964.

———. *US des Soeurs Converses de l'Ordre des Cisterciens Reformes.* Westmalle, 1948.

———. *Regulations of the Order of Cistercians of the Strict Observance.* Dublin, 1926.

———. *Minutes of the Sessions: the Sixtieth General Chapter, Regional Conference, U.S.A.* n.c., 1967.

Rijnberk, G. van. *Le Langage par Signes chez les Moines.* Amsterdam, 1954.

Saint Basil. *Ascetical Works,* translated by Sister M. Monica Wagner. New York, 1950.

Saint Benedict. *Rules for Monasteries,* translated by Leonard J. Doyle. Collegeville, Minnesota, 1948.

Saint Pachomius. *Rule of St Pachomius, Latin Text of Saint Jerome,* edited by A. Boon. Louvain, 1932.

Schaff, Philip and Ware, Henry, edited and translated. *The Nicene and Post-*

Nicene Fathers of The Christian Church, second series, vol. XI. Grand Rapids, Michigan, 1955.

Stolz, Anselme. *L'Ascèse Chrétienne*. Edition des Bénédictines d'Amay, 1948.

Symons, Thomas, editor. *Regularis Concordia: The Monastic Agreement*. London, 1953.

Vilanova, Dom J. Evangelista M., editor. *Regulari Pauli et Stephani*. Abadía de Montserrat, 1959.

Vuillemey, Paul. *La Pensée et les Signes autres que ceux de la Langue*. Paris, 1940.

Wolter, Maurus. *The Principles of Monasticism*, translated and edited by Bernard A. Sause, OSB, St Louis and London, 1962.

Zeller, Hubert van. *Approach to Monasticism*. New York, 1960.

Articles

Buyssens, Eric. "Le langage par gestes chez les moines." *Revue de l'Institute de Sociologie*, XXIX (1956), 537–545.

Dimier, Anselme. "Ars Signorum Cisterciensium." *Collectanea Ordinis Cisterciensium*, V (1938), 165–186.

———. "Observances Monastiques." *Analecta Sacri Ordinis Cisterciensis*, XI (1955), 149–198; especially Part I: Le silence, pp. 160–168.

Gougard, L. "Le Langage des Silencieux." *Revue Mabillon*, XIX (1929), 93–100.

Griesser, Bruno. "Ungedruckte Texte zur Zeichensprache in den Klostern." *Analecta Sacri Ordinis Cisterciensis*, III (1947), 111–137.

Hutt, Clelia. "Etude d'un corpus: Dictionnaire du langage gestuel chez les Trappistes." *Langages*, X (1968), 107–118.

Martins, Mari . "Livros de sinais dos cisterciensis portugueses." *Boletim de Filologia*, XVII (1958 [1960]), 293–357.

Muller, Gregor. "Die Zeichensprache in den Klostern." *Cisterciensen Chronik*, XXI (August, 1909), 243–246.

Neumann, G. "Gesten und Gebärden in der grieschischen Kunst." Review in *American Journal of Archaeology*, LXXI (January, 1967), 106–107, by M. C. Hauser.

Penna, Mario. "I Signa Loquendi Cisterciensis in un Codice della Biblioteca Nacional de Madrid," in *Saggi e Ricerche in memoria de Ettore Li Gotti*, vol. II, 487–521. Palermo, 1962.

Rijnberk, G. van. "De Gebarentaal in een Cistercienserklooster der Nederlanden in de 15e eeuw." *Citeaux*, II (1951). 55–68.

Saint Joseph's Abbey. "Authorized List of Common and Uncommon Signs for St Joseph's Abbey." Spencer, Mass., n.d. (Typewritten).

Schmitz, G. "Die Gebärdensprache der Klunianser und Hirsauer." *Blätter für*

Taubstummenbildung, XXXVI (1923), 347–355; 362–364.

Udalricus of Cluny. "Antiquiores Consuetudines Cluniacensis," in *Patrologiae Cursus Completus*, edited by J. P. Migne, Series Latina, vol. 149, cols. 699–730. Paris, 1882.

GESTURES–LINGUISTICS

Books

Adams, Florence. *Gesture and Pantomimic Action*. Albany, New York, 1891.

Allport, G. W. and Vernon, Philip. *Studies in Expressive Movement*. New York, 1932.

Basham, A. L. *The Wonder that Was India*. New York, 1959.

Bhavani, Enakshi. *The Dance in India*. Bombay, 1965.

Birdwhistell, Ray L. *Introduction to Kinesics*. Louisville, 1952.

Bolinger, Dwight. *Aspects of Language*. New York, 1968.

Clark, William Philo. *The Indian Sign Language*. Philadelphia, 1884.

Cocchiara, Giuseppe. *Il Linguaggio del Gesto*. Turin, 1932.

Cody, Iron Eyes. *How: Sign Talk in Pictures*. Hollywood, California, 1952.

Cohen, Marcel *Pour une Sociologie du Langage*. Paris, 1957.

Coomaraswamy, Ananda. *The Dance of Siva: Fourteen Indian Essays*. New York, 1918.

———— and Gopalakrishnayya, translators. *Nandikesvara: The Mirour of Gesture*, 2nd edition. Cambridge, England, 1936.

Critcheley, Macdonald. *The Language of Gesture*. London, 1939.

Feldman, S. *Mannerisms of Speech and Gesture*. New York, 1959.

Frisch, Karl von. *The Dancing Bees*. New York, 1935.

Ganguly, A. Baram. *Sixty-Four Arts in Ancient India*. New Delhi, 1962.

Hadley, Lewis F. *Indian Sign Talk*. Chicago, 1893.

Hall, Edward T. *The Silent Language*. New York, 1959.

Hughes, John P. *The Science of Language: An Introduction to Linguistics*. New York 1962.

Johanneson, Alexander. *Gestural Origin of Language*. Reykjavik and London, 1952.

————. *Origin of Language*. Reykjavik, 1949.

Kahn, David. *The Codebreakers*. New York, 1968.

Laguna, Grace Andrus de. *Speech: Its Function and Development*. Bloomington, Indiana, 1963.

Lutz, Florence. *The Technique of Pantomime*. Berkeley, 1927.

Mallery, Garrick. *A Collection of Gesture-Signs and Signals of the North American Indians with Some Comparisons.* Miscellaneous Publications, No. 1, Bureau of (Indian) Ethnology, Washington, D.C., 1880.

————. *Introduction to the Study of Sign Languages among North American Indians as Illustrating the Gesture Speech of Mankind.* Bureau of (Indian) Ethnology, Washington, D.C., 1880.

————. *Sign Language among North American Indians.* 1st Annual Report, Bureau of (Indian) Ethnology, Washington, D.C., 1881.

Michel, Charles, L'Abbé de l'Epée. *L'instruction des Sourds et Muets, par Voie des Signes Méthodiques.* Paris, 1776.

Nawab, Vidya Sarabha. 419 *Illustrations of Indian Music and Dance in Western Indian Style.* Ahmedabad, 1964.

Paget, Sir Richard. *Babel, or the Past, Present, and Future of Human Speech.* London, 1930.

————. *Human Speech.* New York and London, 1930.

Pei, Mario. *Invitation to Linguistics.* Garden City, New York, 1965.

————. *The Story of Language.* Philadelphia, 1949.

Ruesch, Jurgen and Kees, W. *Non-Verbal Communication.* Berkeley and Los Angeles, 1956.

Sapir, Edward. *Language: An Introduction to the Study of Speech.* New York, 1921.

Sebeok, Thomas, Hayes, F., and Bateson, Mary (eds). *Approaches to Semiotics.* The Hague, 1964.

Stokoe, William, Jr. *Sign Language Structure: An Outline of the Visual Communication Systems of the American Deaf. Studies in Linguistics,* Occasional Paper No. 8, Buffalo, 1960.

Taylor, Archer. *The Shanghai Gesture.* Folklore Fellows Communications No. 166. Helsinki, 1956.

Tomkins, William. *Universal Indian Sign Language.* San Diego, 1926.

Tylor, Edward B. *Primitive Culture,* 2 vols., 4th edition, Revised. London, 1903.

————. *Researches into the Early History of Mankind.* New York, 1878.

Venkatachalam, Govindraj. *Dance in India.* Bombay, n.d.

Articles

Barakat, Robert A. "Gesture Systems." *Keystone Folklore Quarterly,* XIV (Fall, 1969), 105–121.

Birdwhistell, Ray L. "Background to Kinesics." *Etc.,* XIII (1955), 10–18.

————. "Some Relations between American Kinesics and Spoken American

English," 182–189 in *Communication and Culture*, edited by Alfred G. Smith. New York, 1966.

Davidson, Levette J. "Some Current Folk Gestures and Sign Languages." *American Speech*, XXV (1950), 3–9.

Devereaux, G. "Some Mohave Gestures." *American Anthropologist*, LI (April, 1949), 325–326.

Hapgood, R. "Speak Hands for Me: Gesture as Language in *Julius Caesar*." *Drama Survey*, LIII (Summer, 1966), 162–170.

Hayes, Francis. "Gestures: A Working Bibliography." *Southern Folklore Quarterly*, XXI (December, 1957), 218–317.

Hewes, G. T. "World Distribution of Certain Postural Habits." *American Anthropologist*, LVII (1955), 231–244.

Kakumasu, Jim. "Urubu Sign Language." *International Journal of American Linguistics*, XXXIV (October, 1968), 275–281.

Knowlson, J. R. "Idea of Gesture as a Universal Language in the XVIIth and XVIIIth Centuries." *Journal of the History of Ideas*, XXVI (October, 1965), 495–508.

Kroeber, A. L. "Sign Language Inquiry." *International Journal of American Linguistics*, XXIV (1958), 1–19.

Krout, Maurice. "Understanding Human Gestures. *Scientific Monthly*, XLIX (1939), 167–172.

LaBarre, Weston. "Paralinguistics, Kinesics, and Cultural Anthropology," 191–220, in *Approaches to Semiotics*, edited by Thomas Sebeok *et al* The Hague, 1964.

————. "The Cultural Basis of Emotions and Gestures." *Journal of Personality*, XVI (1947), 49–68.

Lamb, W. "To Make a Gesture." *20th Century*, CLXXVII (1968), 30–33.

Ljung, Magnus. "Principles of a Stratificational Analysis of the Plains Indian Sign Language." *International Journal of American Linguistics*, XXXI (1965), 119–127.

Loomis, G. "Sign Language of Truck Drivers." *Western Folklore*, V (1956), 205–216.

Lyall, A. "Italian Sign Language". *20th Century*. CLIX (1956), 600–604.

Pack, R. "Catullus, Carmen V: Abacus or Finger–Counting." *American Journal of Philology*, LXXVII (June, 1956), 47–51.

Paget, Sir Richard. "Origin of Language, Gesture Theory." *Science*, XCIX (January 7, 1944), 14–15.

Phillot, D. C. "A Note on the Sign, Code and Secret Languages, etc., amongst the Persians." *Journal and Proceedings, Royal Asiatic Society of Bengal*, N.S., III (1907), 619–622.

———. "A Note on the Mercantile Sign Language of India." *Journal and Proceedings, Royal Asiatic Society of Bengal*, N S., III (1906), 333–334.

Richardson, L. J. "Digital Reckoning among the Ancients." *American Mathematical Monthly*, XXIII (1916), 7–13.

Sanford, Eva Matthews. "De Loquela Digitorum." *The Classical Journal*, XXIII (1928), 588–593.

Scott, Hugh L. "The Sign Language of the Plains Indians." *International Folk-lore Association Archives*, I (1893), 1–206.

Siegal, J. P. "Enlightenment and the Evolution of a Language of Signs in France and England." *Journal of the History of Ideas*, XXX (January, 1969), 96–115.

Sullivan, Francis A. "Tendere Manus: Gestures in *The Aeneid*." *The Classical Journal*, LXIII (May, 1968), 358–362.

Trager, George L. "Paralanguage: A First Approximation." *Studies in Linguistics*, XIII (1958), 1–12.

Vendryes, J. "Langage Oral et Langage par Gestes." *Journal de Psychologie Normal et Pathologique*, XLIII (1950), 7–33.

Voegelin, C. F. "Sign Language Analysis, on One Level or Two?" *International Journal of American Linguistics*, XXIV (1958), 71–77.

Walker, Jerell R. "Sign Language of the Plains Indians." *Chronicles of Oklahoma*, XXXI (1953), 168–177.

Wescott, Roger W. "Strepital Communication: A Study of Non-Verbal Sound-Production. Among Men and Animals." *The Bulletin*, New Jersey Academy of Science, XII (Spring, 1967), 30–34.

THE CISTERCIAN FATHERS

NEW ENGLISH TRANSLATIONS
INTRODUCTIONS—NOTES—INDEXES

New English translations of the great Cistercian writers of the Twelfth Century, based on the recently established critical editions, with introductions, notes and indexes, prepared by competent scholars.

CF 1 Bernard of Clairvaux, Vol. 1: *Treatises I*
      Introductions: Jean Leclercq OSB

CF 2 Aelred of Rievaulx, Vol. 1: *Treatises, Pastoral Prayer*
      Introduction: David Knowles

CF 3 William of St Thierry, Vol. 1: *On Contemplating God, Prayer, Meditations*
      Introductions: Jacques Hourlier OSB

CF 4 Bernard of Clairvaux, Vol. 2: *On the Song of Songs I*
      Introduction: Corneille Halflants OCSO

CF 5 Aelred of Rievaulx, Vol. 2: *Spiritual Friendship*
      Introduction: Douglas Roby

CF 6 William of St Thierry, Vol. 2: *Exposition on the Song of Songs*
      Introduction: J. M. Déchanet OSB

CF 7 Bernard of Clairvaux, Vol. 3: *On the Song of Songs II*
      Introduction: Jean Leclercq OSB

CF 8 Guerric of Igny: *Liturgical Sermons I*
      Introduction: Hilary Costello and John Morson OCSO

CF 9 William of St Thierry, Vol. 3: *The Enigma of Faith*
      Introduction: John Anderson

CF 12 William of St Thierry, Vol. 4: *The Golden Epistle*
      Introduction: J. M. Déchanet OSB

CF 13 Bernard of Clairvaux, Vol. 5: *Treatises II*
      Introduction: M. Basil Pennington OCSO

CF 24 *Three Treatises on Man: A Cistercian Anthropology*
      Introduction: Bernard McGinn

CF 32 Guerric of Igny: *Liturgical Sermons II*

CISTERCIAN PUBLICATIONS
Kalamazoo, Michigan